Bermuda

Bermuda

Original text by Ken Bernstein
Revised by Lindsay Bennett
Edited by Richard Wallis
Photography: Pete Bennett except for pages 86, 92, 93, 100 (Jürg Donatsch) and pages 90-91
Cover photograph by Pete Bennett
Photo Editor: Naomi Zinn
Layout: Media Content Marketing, Inc.
Cartography by Ortelius Design
Managing Editor: Tony Halliday

Eleventh Edition 2003

NO part of this book may be reproduced, stored in a retrieval system or transmitted in any form or means electronic, mechanical, photocopying, recording or otherwise, without prior written permission from Apa Publications. Brief text quotations with use of photographs are exempted for book review purposes only.

CONTACTING THE EDITORS
Every effort has been made to provide accurate information in this publication, but changes are inevitable. The publisher cannot be responsible for any resulting loss, inconvenience or injury. We would appreciate it if readers would call our attention to any errors or outdated information by contacting Berlitz Publishing, PO Box 7910, London SE1 1WE, England. Fax: (44) 20 7403 0290;
e-mail: berlitz@apaguide.demon.co.uk

All Rights Reserved
© 2003 Apa Publications GmbH & Co. Verlag KG, Singapore Branch, Singapore

Printed in Singapore by Insight Print Services (Pte) Ltd, 38 Joo Koon Road, Singapore 628990. Tel: (65) 6865-1600. Fax: (65) 6861-6438

Berlitz Trademark Reg. U.S. Patent Office and other countries. Marca Registrada. Used under licence from the Berlitz Investment Corporation

010/311 REV

CONTENTS

● A (☛) in the text denotes a highly recommended sight

Bermuda

BERMUDA AND ITS PEOPLE

The island of Bermuda—which has become synonymous with vacationing—appears on any list of dream destinations drawn up by travel magazines. This geological marvel, a tiny piece of land surrounded by the dark waters of the Atlantic Ocean, sits at the head of the remains of a large volcano which last erupted over 35 million years ago. Like a rocky iceberg, it reaches up from a sea bed about 3,660 m (12,000 ft) deep.

But this is not the reason that Bermuda is on everyone's holiday wish list. To these basic ingredients, nature added a bonus. The warm tradewinds, which rush up from the equatorial regions and blow from west to east across the Atlantic, grace Bermuda with their temperate zephyrs. Although it lies only 918 km (570 miles) from New York, at the same latitude as Cape Hat-

> English is the official language of Bermuda, often spoken with a mid-Atlantic accent. You will hear some colloquial Caribbean speech as well.

teras, North Carolina, it remains warm even in the depths of winter. And these shallow warm seas support the northernmost coral reef in the world.

The shallow reefs and millennia of wave action have created sublimely fine sand beaches, tinged pink by coral and perfect for relaxing. The seas of the inner reef range from the delicate color of green jade to a cornflower blue and are some of the clearest in the world—the perfect environment for diving, snorkeling, or boating on the surface. And down below, creatures of the sea abound in this tiny haven in the deep Atlantic.

The warm winter weather and short flying time make Bermuda the ideal escape from the bitter cold of New York

The well-dressed Bermudian man knows that short hemlines are always in style.

or Boston. Hot but not stifling summer weather invites rest and relaxation, and Bermuda always provides the best in sporting activities, from golf to tennis to long walks on the sand.

Bermuda is not just one island; it is a collection of about 180 named bodies of land, some just big enough for a bird to nest. Only 20 are inhabited, and the seven principal islands are linked by causeways and bridges. The largest island, Grand Bermuda, is 23 km (14 miles) long and gives its name to the whole group, but most also have individual names handed down by settlers and explorers.

Bermuda is the winter home for many migratory bird species, making it a bird-watcher's delight. It is also a refueling stop on the paths of whales, sharks, turtles, and many other species as they travel across the vast ocean, attracting fishermen to enjoy the bounty. Humans appear to have been almost the last species to discover the joys of Bermuda. Early sailors had called it the "Isles of Devils" and went out of their way to avoid it. The island was not named until 1503; Europeans first settled there over a century later. The British claimed her and found the perfect stepping stone to its colonies in the New World. When those colonies achieved independence, Britain used Bermuda as a strategic outpost, creating a "Gibraltar of the West" to match its fortress island in the Mediterranean.

Bermuda has remained British ever since. In fact, with the return of Hong Kong to China in 1997, it has become the largest of Britain's remaining "dependent territories," as they are officially known. There are echoes of the empire and the settlers' way of life found all over the island. Streets with 17th-century buildings and a phalanx of military forts hark back to the birth of Bermudian society. Many of the islands' traditions and quirks are in some ways more British than in the mother-land. Afternoon tea on the terrace and dressing for dinner are both normal practices here. The national game is cricket. State and social occasions are a chance for the whole community to come together, and the white-wigged judges in court and kilted marching bands of the summer parades and tattoos could be in Westminster—if it weren't for the sunshine.

However, Bermuda must also live in today's world. This has brought change to an island more comfortable with the proper (or perhaps that should read the "old") way of doing things. The influence of her close neighbor, the US, has begun to bend the stiff upper lip and chip slowly away at the traditional reserve.

Bermuda Shorts

The national dress for Bermudian males includes Bermuda shorts, worn with panache and found nowhere else in the world. The formal shorts are as tailored as suit trousers and must be no more than 3 inches above the knee. They are worn with long socks (reaching just below the knee) and smart shoes. Topping the whole ensemble are a shirt, tie, and jacket or blazer—just the ticket for the "man about town."

Ties with the eastern US seaboard have always been strong, both with trade and intermarriage, and Bermudian families have on occasion had hard decisions to make when the British Crown fought with their kinsmen. However, the British also invited American involvement on Bermuda through two world wars and in fact leased a large amount of land on Bermuda to the US military for bases in 1940. In 1972, Bermuda made the decision to link its currency to the US dollar. The vast majority of visitors to Bermuda now make the crossing east from the US rather than west from Britain, as Bermuda extends a permanently firm and friendly handshake with its US cousin.

These long and steady relationships have in part helped to create one of the safest vacation destinations you can find; a peaceful and happy society with a high standard of living and little unemployment. Bermuda's stability has made it one of the most secure and most fashionable offshore banking centers in the world, highly regarded for its skill, discretion, and ethical standards. Large amounts of money flow into the island on a daily basis, making it a haven for the "super rich."

Bermuda's waterfront neighborhoods boast brightly painted homes.

Yet this has not altered the basic attitude and approach of the people here. Bermuda is still a conservative island, "charming" in an age when the word has almost been overused. The houses are neat and come in colors from pink to puce, cochineal to canary yellow. Some residents give their homes such whimsical names as "Random Heights" and "On the Rocks." The narrow roads weave across the countryside. Lawns are manicured and watered, with tended flower beds. The streets are kept spotless.

The people, too, are charming; old-fashioned good manners are still the norm here and everyone is unerringly polite.

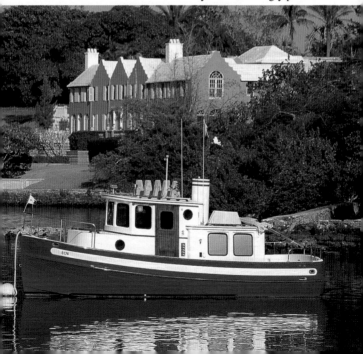

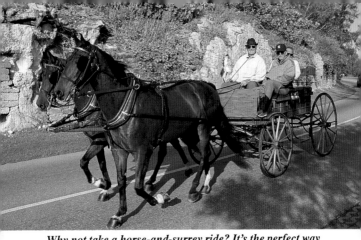

Why not take a horse-and-surrey ride? It's the perfect way to survey all of "charming" Bermuda.

Bermudians will go out of their way to be helpful and pass the time of day with total strangers as if they were neighbors. Big city insularity is an alien concept, but, conversely, so is first name familiarity. Acquaintances are always addressed as "Mr.", "Mrs.," or "Miss" even in informal conversation.

Bermuda's population is approximately 60,000, of whom a bit more than 60 percent are black. Their ancestors were slaves imported centuries ago from the West Indies and Africa as well as later migrants from the Caribbean. There is also a sizeable population of residents of British, Canadian, and US origins. Another significant immigration began in the 19th century, when farmers and gardeners arrived from islands much farther east in the Atlantic—the Azores; some of their descendants still speak a mid-ocean version of Portuguese. A small community of Native American (Pequot) ancestry still lives on St. David's Island.

Meanwhile, 600,000 visitors annually swell the natural population ten times over, maintaining Bermuda's popularity as an almost year-round tourist destination. Many arrive on cruise ships, making forays of exploration from their floating "palaces"; others stay in one of the fine hotels built to take advantage of the sandy bays surrounding the island. Bermudians have worked hard and smart to provide everything a discerning visitor might want. Championship golf courses, sailing clubs, regattas, and hundreds of tennis courts and swimming pools cater to the sports-minded. Shops stocking the finest clothing and gemstones, and a plethora of galleries and independent boutiques allow visitors to shop to their hearts' content. Add to this the many opportunities for fine wining and dining worthy of Paris, and you have the perfect recipe for a little pampered "R&R."

> **The always-courteous Bermudians might greet you by saying "All right," for they assume you meant to ask, "How do you do?"**

Visitors come for the special atmosphere that could only be Bermuda: British tradition mixed with West Indian ingredients, topped with a twist of Americana. They come because there are no shocks or surprises in store. Bermuda is a little like an old armchair into which you know you can settle down and get really comfortable. It's going to make you feel warm and cozy, and it's soft and tame. Those who want the excitement and frisson of the unknown or unfamiliar—perhaps a little lively underground "street" life—might want to look elsewhere, perhaps in those noisy towns of the Caribbean that Bermuda tries so hard to distance itself from. Bermuda wants to be your home away from home, not the adventure of a lifetime.

As Mark Twain once wrote, "Go to heaven if you want to. I'd rather stay here in Bermuda." He was beguiled by its charms, just as you will be.

A BRIEF HISTORY

This remote group of islands remained unnamed until it was spotted by Spanish navigator Juan Bermúdez in 1503. Only a few years later an Italian map showed "La Bermuda." It was also called the "Isles of Devils" because early navigators were terrified of Bermuda's reefs and celebrated their salvation when they had passed safely by. Despite benign conditions and ample food, there were few visitors, and those who landed did so usually because they were shipwrecked. One was the anonymous sailor who carved the date 1543 on a rock on the south coast, now known as Spanish Rock. He also inscribed a cross and a pair of letters, perhaps his initials or those of his king.

The Sea Venture

In 1606 James I granted a charter to the Virginia Company to establish the first English colony in America, named Jamestown in the king's honor. Three years later a second contingent of settlers set sail from Plymouth under Admiral Sir George Somers. Less than halfway across the Atlantic, the fleet ran into a vicious storm. The flagship vessel, called *Sea Venture*, was separated from the rest of the convoy and eventually snagged on the reefs just east of Bermuda on 28 July 1609.

Historical Fiction?

At the time of Sir George Somers' shipwreck in 1609, an English playwright was looking for a new story. As news of the great storm and the fate suffered by the *Sea Venture* on the reefs of Bermuda reached England, he saw it as just the incident to enliven his plot. William Shakespeare's next play was, of course, *The Tempest*, first performed in 1611.

Miraculously, all aboard were ferried to shore. It turned out that Bermuda was an ideal place to be stranded. After less than a year, Somers and his group had built new ships from local cedar and timber salvaged from the remains of the *Sea Venture.* Leaving behind only two men, the Somers party resumed their journey westward and finally landed at Jamestown, only to be greeted by a shock: illness, starvation, and Indian attacks had drastically decimated the colony. Somers set sail almost immediately, headed back to Bermuda. He knew that it could provide the people of Jamestown with enough food to save them from further hardship. Unfortunately, he died trying to organize the Bermuda-Jamestown lifeline. His body was shipped back to England but his heart was buried in Bermuda, the colony he would later be credited with founding.

King James added the name of Bermuda to the original Virginia Company Charter, and in the spring of 1612 more than 50 colonists were sent out on the *Plough* to join three pioneers who had volunteered to hold the fort. Defenses were built and the town of St. George's was established at the east end of Bermuda,

Sir George Somers' memorial in Bermuda, where he (literally) left his heart.

Historical Landmarks

1503 Spanish explorer Juan Bermúdez is credited with being the first to sight and record the existence of the islands.

1609 Admiral Sir George Somers sets out for Virginia but is shipwrecked on Bermuda's reefs. A settlement eventually develops.

1612 The Bermuda Company is created to run the island.

1615 Right of self-government is granted.

1775 Bermuda sides with American colonies against British rule.

1815 Bermuda's capital is moved from St. George to Hamilton.

1834 Slavery is abolished. Emancipation of slaves

1872 First steamship service between New York and Bermuda.

1917 US navy leases White's Island during World War I to be used as a base to chase German submarines.

1941 US Air Force bases built on land leased for 99 years.

1957 British garrison withdrawn from Bermuda.

1968 In the first elections under new Bermuda Constitution, the United Bermuda Party is elected to govern.

1971 Sir Edward Richards becomes Bermuda's first black premier.

1972 Bermuda allies its currency to the US dollar.

1998 The Progressive Labour Party wins general elections, breaking over thirty years of rule by the United Bermuda Party.

2003 Celebration of the 400th anniversary of the "discovery" of Bermuda by Jaun de Bermudez.

near the spot where the *Sea Venture* castaways had first landed. The Bermuda Company was then created to administer the island.

News of the British settlement agitated the Spanish. After all, a Spaniard had discovered (and given his name to) Bermuda. Philip III of Spain was urged by his advisors to act immediately to force the British out. Two ships were dispatched with orders to evaluate the situation. As they approached the island, the small British population created a number of ruses to convince the Spanish that Bermuda was well defended; two salvos fired from a cannon went across the bay. The Spanish fell for the ploy and fled, grossly overestimating the strength of the English garrison, which couldn't have mustered a third shot at that time. Bermuda's Britishness was affirmed.

A Growing Colony

Progress was swift during the first few years of the colony's existence. In 1619 the congregation of St. Peter's Church moved into a permanent building, and Bermuda's parliament met in an enclosure still visible amid the pews. But it was soon decided to separate the secular from the religious, and a new government building went up. State House, Bermuda's first stone structure, is still standing today in St. George.

An English surveyor, Richard Norwood, undertook a study of the terrain, dividing the colony into the nine "tribes" that are the parishes (counties) of today and the origin of the numerous "Tribe Roads" still to be seen across the island. Of the nine parishes, all but St. George's were named after prominent shareholders in the original Bermuda Company.

During this period local money was minted, called "Hog" money after the wild pig on the reverse side; it was Britain's first colonial currency. Agriculture was to be the economic base for the new colony, whose major crop was tobacco. In reality, Bermuda could never compete with the crops produced in Virginia, but it began to develop a plantation system, including the importation of slave labor. The slaves were treated a bit better than were those on islands farther south, and slavery was finally abolished in Britain (and Bermuda) in 1834. The initial centuries of enforced settlement, followed by emancipation and the ensuing years of equality, have produced Bermuda's modern biracial society.

When agriculture failed to be profitable, the ingenious settlers looked for other ways to make a living. Bermuda sits astride the main whale migration route, and because the motherland and other colonies demanded (and paid well for) the oil,

State House was built in the early 1600s so that parliament could meet somewhere other than in church.

the local population went into the whaling business. Once the colonists were good enough seamen to land whales, it was perhaps only natural that they might turn their skills to another historical marine tradition: piracy. The practice evolved modestly, perhaps even legally, from the salvaging (called "wrecking") of treasure found on ships grounded on the local reefs. From there it was easy to make the transition to taking goods by subterfuge or by force. Smuggling was so commonplace that it passed almost unnoticed.

Changing Loyalties

Isolated from London by more than 5,300 km (3,300 miles) in an age of slow communications, Bermuda sometimes found itself out of step with developments in the homeland. In 1649, the islanders were appalled to learn of the execution of Charles I and the proclamation of Cromwell's Commonwealth. They later rejoiced when Charles II was restored to the throne in 1660.

Another era ended in 1684 when the Bermuda Company lost its charter. After a five-year legal battle, Bermuda became a British colony with a degree of self-government. The authorities in London appointed a Governor to act as the crown representative (this is still the system today). The most difficult test of Bermuda's loyalties came when the American colonies rose in rebellion against George III. London forbade Bermuda to trade with or otherwise support General Washington's revolutionaries. This was a heartbreaking decree for the islanders to obey in light of Bermuda's close personal and family ties with the people of Virginia and other American colonies. Commerce also provided a strong rationale for helping the rebels, for Bermuda received most of its grain from the North American colonies. Simply put, Bermuda needed food and George Washington needed gunpowder.

On a dark night in mid-August 1775, several boats sailed into the dark harbor of Tobacco Bay near Fort St. Catherine and, in a daring and dangerous raid, stole 100 kegs of gunpowder from the main ordnance store. Once safely on the boats, the ammunition made its way to the rebel forces. To this day nobody knows if this was part of an orchestrated campaign or simply a spur-of-the-moment action by local sympathizers. But Bermuda got its grain. The British authorities were horrified but could find no conclusive proof of guilt. The Tuckers, a prominent family with many connections to the American revolutionaries, were the prime suspects. Not all Bermudians, however, were sympathetic to the rebel cause, as privateers continued to capture and ransack American ships.

Gibraltar of the West

With the loss of its naval bases in the American colonies, Britain began to appreciate Bermuda's strategic importance. They wanted to create a "Gibraltar of the West" and set about building a large naval dockyard on Ireland Island, at the opposite end of the archipelago from the main population center of St. George's. The addition of this important facility shifted the center of communications in the colony, prompting authorities to transfer the capital from St. George's to the hitherto undistinguished village of Hamilton. Traditionalists were furious.

Starting in 1824, Britain sent convicts to Bermuda to supplement the slave labor working on the dockyard project. At any given time there were well over 1,000 prisoners employed in the development of the outpost's military potential. Yellow fever, dysentery, and scurvy killed a sizable proportion of these unfortunates, who were crammed into filthy floating prisons (called "hulks") during the hours they weren't working. These hulks were used until 1863.

Bermuda and the US Civil War

Slavery had been abolished in Bermuda more than a quarter-century before the outbreak of the American Civil War, yet islanders' sympathies lay with the South. Although Britain remained officially neutral and British subjects were forbidden from taking part in the hostilities, the Bermudians pitched in to help supply British arms and goods to the Confederate cause against the Union forces.

St. George's Harbour and Penno's Wharf were working at full capacity to unload cargoes that were then transferred onto blockade-runners. These long, slim vessels were specially designed

Gates Fort once guarded St. George's Harbour; it was also once used as a family home.

to outrun the Union navy's picket ships. They made their way to Wilmington, North Carolina, the closest Confederate port to Bermuda. Here they would take on a new cargo of cotton —a most profitable ballast that increased in value tenfold by the time it was delivered to buyers in Britain. St. George's boomed during the Civil War; the town seethed with sailors, speculators, Confederate agents, and Union spies. When General Lee laid down his sword in 1865, it was as if Bermuda, too, had lost a war.

Bermuda's colonial ties with Britian have been sorely tested since World War II.

In the years that followed, Bermuda's fortunes picked up as the first steamships began to arrive on a regular basis. In 1883 Princess Louise (daughter of Queen Victoria) arrived on a lengthy visit en route to her new home farther north, as the wife of the Governor General of Canada. She extolled Bermuda to those in her upper-class English circles, and wealthy tourists began to arrive soon thereafter. By the turn of the century, Bermuda was a well-known winter destination for visitors from the US and Canada as well as Britain. The Princess Hotel was opened in Hamilton in 1885 to commemorate the visit.

Three More Wars

At the turn of the twentieth century, the Boer War (the struggle between British and Dutch settlers in South Africa) sent shock waves as far as Bermuda. Thousands of Boer prisoners were shipped to the colony, and prison camps were established on half-a-dozen islands in Great Sound. After the Boers lost the war, many of the prisoners chose to remain in Bermuda rather than accept a British South Africa.

During World War I, Bermudian volunteers fought in France while others joined resident British forces in defending the islands. German submarines aggravated the supply problem and threatened ships stopping in the islands to refuel for the remainder of the Atlantic crossing. When the Americans entered the conflict, White's Island, just opposite the Hamilton waterfront, was leased to the US government. It was a small-scale preview of the American military presence that would be established in World War II.

Between the two world wars, tourism became a prime economic factor, and luxury cruise liners began regular runs between New York and Bermuda during the 1920s. Resort hotels were built to attract Americans escaping the northern winter (and the Prohibition laws against alcoholic beverages).

When war broke out in Europe in 1939, Bermuda's growing tourist industry all but collapsed. The ships were commandeered to carry troops or become floating hospitals, and the waters around the islands were infested with German submarines. Bermuda played an important role in intelligence. In the basements of the Princess and Bermudiana hotels, more than a thousand British experts analyzed communications intercepted between the western hemisphere and Europe. Mail quietly removed from refueling ships and planes was steamed open and tested for microdots and invisible codes, an important contribution to the struggle against Axis spying activity. The big hotels stayed in business by serving as billets for servicemen and civilian war workers.

Just as the first British M15 intelligence operatives were arriving in Hamilton in August 1940, the Lend-Lease Act was negotiated between Britain and the US. Under a 99-year lease, the US acquired about one-tenth of the land area of Bermuda for the development of naval and air bases, modernizing the defenses of Britain's "Gibraltar of the West."

Changing Times

In the years after World War II, the centuries-old links with Britain began to change. The "Imperial" coffers were empty, the empire swiftly began to contract, and British military forces were pulled out of Bermuda after 174 years.

Social changes also began to revolutionize the old way of life. The motor car was introduced, bringing about the demise of the horse-drawn carriage and eventually causing the bankruptcy of the new Bermuda Railway in 1947. The 1950s saw racial segregation end in the major hotels and restaurants (although schools were not integrated until

After nearly 500 years of relative tumult, Bermuda is now enjoying new opportunities and comfortable prosperity.

1971). In 1968, a new constitution was adopted to make self-government more representative and effective; elections were won by the United Bermuda Party. Then suddenly, in 1970, the colony was expelled from the "Sterling area," and Bermuda chose to ally its currency to the US dollar.

These abrupt and far-reaching changes on an island proud of its traditional ways brought strain and conflict. Riots broke out in 1968, and British troops had to be called in to restore order. Five years later the governor, Sir Richard Sharples, and his aide were assassinated. When the alleged assassins were executed in 1977, more riots ensued.

However, Bermuda pulled back from the brink of social chaos and began to return to its peaceful and law-abiding ways. With progressive taxation for its residents, the colony enjoyed one of the highest standards of living in the world. Where whaling and piracy were once important industries, the colony now looked to the less exciting but more predictable earnings from tourism, insurance, and banking enterprises. In the 1970s the number of so-called exempt companies more than doubled, and they now compete with tourism as the major contributor to Bermuda's balance-of-payments' surplus.

The political status quo under the United Bermuda Party continued until November 1998, when the PLP (Progressive Labour Party) won an unexpected landslide victory in the general elections. This not only surprised the old school but ushered in a new era full of opportunity for development as the island keeps up with a rapidly changing world. Challenges include environmental and housing issues as well as problems of unemployment, unknown in modern Bermuda until the final years of the 20th century. Positive long-term solutions will ensure that Bermuda continues to enjoy the wealth, security, and comfort it has created for itself.

WHERE TO GO

Bermuda is a small group of islands and thus relatively easy to explore. Distances are short here, so the unavailability of rental cars (they're off-limits to tourists!) is really a plus. It means you'll be on buses, taxis, bicycles, or mopeds —or on foot—to enjoy Bermuda's many pleasures. And the pace is relaxed; speed limits are only 32 km/h (20 mph).

Around every corner there are beautiful views, elegant architecture, and exquisite natural areas. Combine this with a wealth of historical attractions, museums, forts, and churches, and Bermuda is an explorer's delight. We start our tour at Hamilton, the capital, then travel from this center first to the south and west, and then to the east and north.

The main drag: Hamilton's pretty Front Street is lined with restaurants, shops, and all sorts of pleasant surprises.

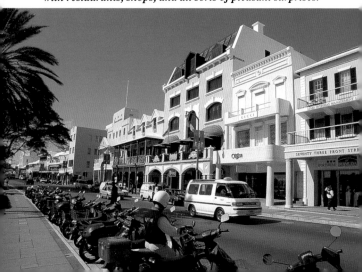

HAMILTON

The capital of Bermuda since 1815, **Hamilton** is a very small and friendly city, despite its importance in the world of finance, banking, and insurance. It is the heart of government and decision making, and because it is the only container port on the island, it is also the center of shipping and trade. Local people gravitate here for shopping and entertainment, and visitors crowd the streets in summer when the cruise ships are in town.

Front Street runs along the water and is the first part of town seen by cruise passengers as ships come to shore. It is the life and soul of Hamilton and a focus for many activities, especially during the summer months. A long row of pastel-painted buildings offer the best in tax-free shopping: jewelry, liquor, clothing, and crystal. Explore the narrow alleyways that lead off Front Street to discover small shops selling collectibles or locally designed arts and crafts, or small restaurants offering local seafood. On Front Street itself there are a number of restaurants with verandas on the first floor, where you can have a drink or meal and watch the world go by. At the west end of Front Street, on the waterfront, you will find the Visitors' Service Bureau and the terminal for the local ferries that ply across Great and Little Sound from Hamilton to the southern and western parts of Bermuda.

> The city of Hamilton has only about 6,000 residents. Surrounding Pembroke Parish adds another 10,000 to the "metropolitan" total.

On summer evenings, Front Street comes alive with Harbour Night. Street performers, craft stalls, and late-night shopping are all part of the festivities. There is also the **Beat Retreat Ceremony**, where the Band and Corps of Drums of the Bermuda Regiment and the Bermuda Islands Pipe Band, in full military dress, march the street to recreate a centuries-old ceremony.

Most of Hamilton's attractions can be seen on foot and would make an enjoyable day's stroll. But there is also the option of taking a carriage ride through the streets—there's nothing more romantic than a horse-drawn carriage taking a stately route. Carriages can be hired on Front Street during the summer season.

On foot, your tour might begin at the head office of the **Bank of Bermuda**, which is on Front Street behind the Ferry Terminal. This is one of the few "high-rise" buildings in Hamilton, as

The "Beat Retreat" Ceremony

The ceremony of "beating retreat" is one of the oldest in British military history, dating back to the 16th century. It is also one of the premier summer attractions on Bermuda.

The event has its origins in the procedures followed at night for closing the town gates when battlements protected both the military and civilian populations. At sunset each day, a bugle was sounded to gather the new guard and to warn all those outside the safety of the walls to return. This was known as "retreat call."

Later, a protocol was formulated to call soldiers back to their barracks at the end of the evening. As drummers walked the streets, the sound of the drums was the signal for publicans to turn off their taps and for soldiers to drink up and head back to base. This happened some hours after the "retreat call" and became known as the "tattoo," a corruption of the phrase "turn off the taps" (here also is the origin of the American military "taps," which signals "lights out").

The Beat Retreat ceremony now combines the two separate functions into one loud and colorful parade—with drums and bagpipes—through the streets of downtown Hamilton.

most of the town's structures are less than three stories in height. The formal façade has a number of heraldic plaques signifying its ancient pedigree. Inside, the bank keeps a collection of rare and valuable coins dating back through Bermuda's history. Every type of coin minted by the British crown can be found here, from the time of James I in 1603 (when the charter was granted that brought Bermuda's first settlers) to the present day, including an example of "Hog" money. Be sure to see the 1887 £5 coin, which caused consternation among British subjects of the time. Because the crown pictured on Queen Victoria's head was far too small, many people thought that the Queen (and, by extension, the empire) looked ridiculous.

Mr. Perot's Post Office, once home base for Bermuda's first Postmaster General.

From the bank, head for **Queen Street**, which leads north from the **Birdcage**, a metal cage once used by police officers to direct the traffic that regularly comes to a halt on Front Street. It was designed by a Mr. Bird, although it also has a resemblance to "Tweetie Bird's" cage. Traffic lights now regulate the junction. Remember to look right as you prepare to cross the road!

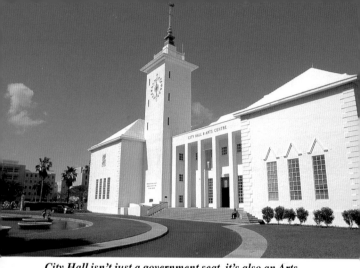

City Hall isn't just a government seat, it's also an Arts Centre housing European and local works.

On the left as you walk up Queen Street is **Perot's Post Office**, named after the man who was appointed Bermuda's first Postmaster General in 1821. He had actually been acting as "unofficial" postman for several years, meeting the ships and putting the letters under his hat before touring the town to deliver them. William B. Perot (pronounced "Pea-rut") went one stage further in 1848 when he began to produce his own postage stamps; only 11 are known to exist today, making each one extremely valuable. The little Post Office is very much as Perot kept it, neat and simply furnished. The building still houses an active post office, which makes it an appropriate place to buy the stamps for your postcards. Bermudian stamps always have a colorful and interesting design; perhaps you can start a collection by buying a set for yourself.

Just behind the Post Office is a building that houses the **Bermuda National Library** and the **Historical Society Museum**, prime collections devoted to important historical documents and artifacts from the island. The public rooms are small but full of Bermudian treasures. Silver, china, coins, and furniture have been gathered together, including rare and valuable "hog" money as well as some of the Confederate notes that were used to pay for goods before the Civil War. Many Bermudian businessmen and sailors were paid in money that became worthless after the Unionists won the war.

The house is set in gardens, now called **Par-la-Ville Park**, that are open to the public daily. Here you will find businessmen eating lunch, chattering school children, and a family of cats who call the place home. Perot planned the gardens during his time at the Post Office, and the spot has changed very little since that time.

Queen Street climbs as far as Church Street, a main east-west thoroughfare named for the many houses of worship located along its course. When you reach Church Street, take

The Confederate Seal

There were no die engravers in the American Confederacy, so the task was left to J. Wyon of London, who was Chief Engraver of Her Majesty's Seals. He engraved a seal that included the date 22 February 1862, commemorating the meeting of the first session of the Confederate Congress. The seal and its press were shipped to Bermuda, where four attempts were made to break the Union blockade before they could be delivered to the Confederate government. Due to the weight, only the seal was finally delivered; the press was left behind in St. George's. This original seal now rests in the Museum of the Confederacy in Richmond, Virginia.

a right turn. A little way up the street on the left is the Hamilton **City Hall and Arts Centre**, a bright white building with a distinctive painted clock on the front facade. It now contains the **Bermuda National Gallery**, built around the Watlington collection of 17th- and 18th-century European paintings by such artists as Joshua Reynolds and Thomas Gainsborough. Also here is The Bermuda Society of Arts, a venue for local artists to display their work, and host to visiting exhibitions.

Next to City Hall is the island's main bus terminal, the hub of Bermuda's public transportation system which is on-time, clean, and efficient. You will see here the boarding locations for the island's various bus routes (see page 124).

Across Victoria Street from the bus terminal is Victoria Park, originally a children's playground but later landscaped to commemorate the Silver Jubilee of Queen Victoria in 1887. The main features are the sunken garden, lawns, and flowerbeds in traditional English style, and the beautiful ornate iron bandstand, where open-air concerts are still performed during the summer and in December just before Christmas.

Return to Church Street and walk east to the **Cathedral of the Most Holy Trinity**, consecrated in 1911 after a fire destroyed the previous edifice in 1884. The style is Early English, with a tower rising 44 m (143 ft) to provide good views of the town. You can climb to the top for a small donation to church funds; the tower is open on weekdays only. Perhaps the most dramatic area in the church is the wall behind the altar, where there are sculptures in niches depicting Christ and the saints. Completed in 1967 it is a fitting modern edition to the church. By contrast, farther along

Well-named Church Street houses the Cathedral of the Most Holy Trinity (right) plus St. Andrew's and Wesley churches.

Church Street is the oldest church in Hamilton, **St. Andrew's Presbyterian Church** (founded in 1843), as well as Wesley Methodist Church.

Across Church Street from Wesley Methodist Church you will find the rear portion of **Sessions House**, home to the Bermuda Assembly and the Supreme Court. Walk down Parliament Street to reach the front of the building. Sessions House dates from 1819, but the Italianate tower, colonnades, and decorative touches were added in 1887 for the Silver Jubilee. Bermuda's parliament is the oldest in the British Commonwealth and is still modeled after its predecessor in London. The **annual opening ceremonies** and the **regular sessions** are open to visitors, who can sit in the public gallery

For a thoroughly British experience, visit Sessions House to watch Bermuda's parliament in action.

to watch the robed and white-wigged Speaker preside over the legislative deliberations (the Assembly meets on Fridays from late October until early July). The Supreme Court can also be viewed and is in session throughout the year.

The home of the Bermuda Senate is farther down Parliament Street at **Cabinet House** (built in 1833), where the premier and cabinet also have offices. The building has welcomed a number of world leaders to its meeting rooms, including Sir Winston Churchill and John F. Kennedy. The ceremonial sword of state, mace, and oar are kept here and used at the opening of parliament, held each year in early November. The opening speech is given from a Bermuda Cedar seat fashioned in 1642, when meetings were still held in St. George's. Bermuda's Senate has no legislative powers and is rather more of a debating forum; its sessions can be observed on Wednesdays.

> The cannons you see at Fort Hamilton once fired 400-pound shells. They were moved here to enhance the sightseeing atmosphere.

Outside the Cabinet building on Front Street is the **Cenotaph**, which commemorates Bermuda's dead of the two World Wars. The monument dates from 1920, its design based on that of the war memorial that stands in London's Whitehall. The solemn ceremonies of Remembrance Day take place here on 11 November each year, when wreaths are laid and silent homage is paid to those who gave their lives.

From Front Street, a ten-minute walk up the steep incline of King Street leads to **Fort Hamilton**, which was built in 1889 to protect the harbor and formed part of a line of defense for the naval dockyard to the west. Today it offers spectacular views over the rooftops of Hamilton, especially thrilling when the cruise ships are in port. The upper levels and battlements have been landscaped with fine lawns, which

BERMUDA HIGHLIGHTS

Note that many sites and attractions are closed on public holidays (see page 121).

Hamilton

Sessions House, *Bermuda Assembly*. Open Monday–Friday 9am–12:30pm, 2–5pm. *Supreme Court*. Open Monday–Friday 8:30am–4:45pm.

Bermuda Senate. Open Monday–Friday 9am–5pm.

Perot Post Office. Open Monday–Friday 9am–5pm.

Bermuda National Library and the Historical Society Museum. Open Monday–Saturday 9:30am–3:30pm.

Bermuda National Gallery (including the Society of Arts Gallery). Open Monday–Saturday 10am–4pm.

Cathedral of the Most Holy Trinity. Open daily 8am–4:45pm. Tower. Open Monday–Friday 10am–3.30pm.

Fort Hamilton. Open daily 9:30am–5pm.

Near Hamilton

Waterville. Open Monday–Friday 9am–5pm.

Camden and Botanical Gardens. Open daily from sunrise until sunset, with tours of the gardens at 10:30am on Tuesday, Wednesday, and Friday.

Arboretum. Open daily from sunrise until sunset.

St. George's

St. Peter's Church. Open daily and for Sunday services.

Bermuda Museum of the National Trust. Open Monday–Saturday 10am–4pm.

Tucker House Museum. Open Monday–Saturday 10am–4pm. (A combination ticket can be bought that covers admission for the National Trust Museum, Tucker House, and Verdmont Museum. The ticket can be purchased at any of the three locations.)

King's Square. Historic re-enactments (town crier, ducking stool, and stocks) at noon: on Monday–Thursday and Saturday from May through October; on Wednesday and Saturday from November through April.

Deliverance. The ship is open daily 9am–5pm from April through November.

Carriage Museum. Open Monday–Friday 10am–4pm.

Featherbed Alley Printery. Open Monday–Friday 10am–4pm from April through October; open Wednesday 11am–3pm November and January to March.

St. George's Historical Society Museum. Open Monday–Friday 10am–4pm from April through October; open Wednesday 11am–3pm November and January through March.

Fort St. Catherine. Open daily 10am–4pm

Near Harrington Sound

Verdmont Museum. Open Tuesday–Saturday 10am–4pm.

Bermuda Aquarium, Museum of Natural History, and Zoo. Open daily 9am–5pm.

Crystal Caves. Open daily 9:30am–4:30pm.

Devil's Hole Aquarium. Open daily 9:30am–4:30pm.

Spittal Pond Nature Reserve. Open daily from sunrise until sunset.

The West End

Dolphin Quest. Programs run daily at the Bermuda Maritime Museum in the Dockyard, for reservations contact tel: 234-4464; fax: 234-4992.

Scaur Hill Fort. Open daily: 9am–4:30pm

Chapel at Heydon Trust. Open daily from dawn until dusk.

Maritime Museum (in the Royal Naval Dockyard). Open 9:30am–4:30pm from April through November; open 10am–4:30pm from December through March.

make a fine place for a summer picnic. Long, cool tunnels in the depths of the defenses were originally dug as a protected route for ammunition replenishment. They also lead to the deep moat, once the first line of protection against manned assault but now converted into a splendid tropical garden with varieties of giant bamboo, fern, and ficus. Creeping plants now climb the sheer walls, providing a new home to numerous birds, lizards, and frogs. Every Monday from November to March, the fort hosts a display by the Bermuda Islands Pipe Band, complete with kilts and highland dancers.

East on Front Street, out of Hamilton yet only a few minutes walk from the shops and restaurants of the town center, is the **Bermuda Underwater Exploration Institute**, which celebrates the important part Bermuda has played in the development of this fledgling science and sport. The building has a light and spacious modern design, offering the chance to wander easily among the exhibits. A short video tells the story of the development of the Bathysphere, a machine that could withstand the immense water pressure thousands of feet beneath the surface so that scientists could study the creatures living at those depths. Displays explain how a seashell is created, and, in the next room, the Stonington Collection comprises 5000 different seashell varieties from around the world, including many found in waters off Bermuda. The sheer variety and beauty are breathtaking.

The finale of your visit to the Institute is a simulated trip aboard a deep-sea exploration vessel that transports you 3,660 m (about 12,000 ft) under sea, the approximate depth of the Atlantic in the waters surrounding Bermuda's shallow coral reefs. The introduction to the "dive" paints a vivid picture of the geology of Bermuda and its incredible position in the middle of this vast, deep ocean. Your journey leads through re-creations of the environments found at several dif-

Seashells from Bermuda and other far-off lands are displayed at the Underwater Exploration Institute.

ferent ocean layers, then on to displays of treasure salvaged from wrecks around the island. The whole exhibit makes you appreciate the work of the ferry pilots who guide ships in and out of the treacherous reefs surrounding Bermuda.

Spanish Point

Northwest of the city of Hamilton, in Pembroke Parish, lies a small area of land reaching out into the mouth of Great Sound. Vehicles reach this area through Black Watch Pass, a cutting through the high coral cliff that was opened in 1934. Over 2.5 million tons of rock were removed to create the first route over the North Shore Cliffs. The road (bus route #4) ends at **Spanish Point** and the small Stovel Bay, where there is a picturesque park with views of the distant dock-

Waterville, dating from the 18th century but lived in until fairly recently, offers a peek into the Bermudian good life.

yard across the strait. An intriguing wreck lies at Spanish Point, part of the floating dock (the second largest in the world) that once sat at the Royal Naval Dockyard. It was being towed out of the harbor for scrap but broke loose from its ties and foundered on rocks here, never to be moved again.

SOUTH AND WEST FROM HAMILTON

The journey out of Hamilton to the south leads through the parishes of Paget, Warwick, and Southampton before reaching Sandys Parish, where the "hook" of Bermuda curves up to Somerset and Ireland islands. The south coast has miles of sublime pink-sand beaches and a reef wall that parallels the coastline. After the spectacular panorama viewed from

Gibb's Hill Lighthouse (on one of Bermuda's highest points), the land narrows to a string of small islands held together by a series of small bridges leading eventually to the sites of Britain's former glory.

Leave Hamilton by traveling east on Front Street—with the harbor on your right—until you reach a traffic circle (roundabout). Take the "Foot of the Lane," then turn onto Pomander Road to reach **Waterville**, a historic home and now headquarters for the Bermuda National Trust. The home belonged to the Trimingham family, prominent business people and traders who still operate the best-known department store chain on the island. James Harvey Trimingham began trading from the Waterville site in 1842 and opened the Front Street Store (still in business) in 1861. The house, one of the oldest on Bermuda, was built around 1725 on land bought by John Trimingham II. Originally, the family built ships and operated a wharf in front of the house, "at the foot of the Lane," as the end of Hamilton Harbour was then known. The bottom floor of the house was used to store goods and equipment, while the upper floor provided living quarters. In 1961 the house was acquired by the Historic Monuments Trust, precursor to the Bermuda National Trust, but it was still occupied by elderly Trimingham family members until 1990. Two rooms on the upper level are open to the public, where Trimingham furniture and family portraits can be seen. Just as popular are the gardens, set against the water's edge. A 300-year-old tamarind tree sheds comforting shade over the house, and ducks come from the water to share your sandwiches.

If you turn up Berry Hill Road at the same roundabout, you will find the entrance to the Botanical Gardens and Camden (bus route #1). **Camden** was designated as the official residence of Bermuda's premier after self-government began in 1970. It is an impressive colonial building with painted shutters and fretwork. The **Botanical Gardens** that surround the house were inaugurated in 1898 and doubled in size to 15 hectares (36 acres) in 1921. There are large glass houses with cacti and orchids along with formal gardens, lawns, and an aromatic garden designed for the enjoyment of blind visitors. There are also tables under the trees in the rolling landscape in front of Camden for picnics. The whole area is a delight for plant lovers and anyone else who wants a pleasant spot to relax.

Leaving Hamilton

You can take three main routes to travel south and west along Bermuda's "fish-hook." The northernmost (called most appropriately Harbour Road) leads along the south shore of Hamilton Harbour, with views of the islands that lie scattered in Great Sound and make navigation into the cruise port so tricky. A number of ferry terminals on the Hamilton-Warwick and Hamilton-Paget routes can be found on Harbour Road, as can many hotels and guest houses, away from the bustle of Hamilton but within easy reach of all its facilities.

"Duck Island" is at the innermost part of Hamilton Harbour. Here the ducks—like Bermuda's tourists— enjoy basking in the sun.

The middle route (up Crow Lane and Stowe Hill to Middle Road) is the most direct if you are in a hurry. It leads past the Belmont Country Club and Hotel, with its fine golf course, and later passes the Waterlot Inn, one of the finest restaurants on the island. The building is from the 17th century and occupies a setting at the head of a pretty bay (bus route #8).

The most southerly road (South Road) is the most scenic and leads to some of the best beaches and finest resorts on Bermuda (bus route #7).

The South Road

You will come first to the **Elbow Beach Resort** and the nearby public Bermuda Beach. The resort is one of the premier hotels on the island and sits on a long stretch of sand that is for hotel guests exclusively. South Road travels on top of the cliffs and offers beautiful views of the sand dunes and beaches below. Don't worry about trying to take in these views while driving, for there are many stopping places along the way where you can take photographs or simply enjoy the panorama. The way to each beach is marked with a wooden sign, which leads to parking areas for bicycles and cars off the main road.

By Moped Around Bermuda

No rental cars. Gorgeous weather. Quiet roads. Relatively flat surfaces. What better way to explore tiny Bermuda than on a moped? Puttering around the islands can be exhilarating, but don't dash off on your rented motorbike until you've read the following tips:

- Be sure the rental agency explains the machine and you fully understand how to start, drive, and stop it. Test drive your moped under supervision until you feel confident.
- You must wear the helmet provided.
- Dress for comfort and protection: no bathing suits, no bare feet. Wear proper shoes rather than sandals, and take along a windbreaker. Sunglasses are good protection against flying insects and gravel. Sunscreen is a must.
- Keep reminding yourself to drive on the left, especially at traffic circles (roundabouts)—where traffic moves clockwise.
- Keep eyes front, and don't worry about traffic behind you. The locals approach tourists with caution!
- When you're not on the bike, lock it.

Horse fanciers can take a romantic ride along the water in South Shore Park, Warwick Long Bay.

Once you reach **Warwick Long Bay** there are a series of public beaches that allow you to walk along the sand or find a patch to call your own for the day. Miles of footpaths in the dunes and undulating grassland behind the beaches have been designated as **South Shore Park**. These areas are perfect for walking, jogging, or horseback riding.

The most southerly of the beaches fronting South Shore Park is **Horseshoe Bay**, one of the prettiest and most photographed on Bermuda. A crescent of fine pink-tinged sand with good facilities including a restaurant/café, it makes a good starting or finishing point for your explorations.

The next bay to Horseshoe Bay is **East Whale Bay**, the private beach of the Fairmont Southampton Princess Hotel, which sits majestically on the hills above. From the main road the hotel is easily seen with its pale pink color. Below are the greens and fairways of the Princess's executive golf course.

Best Beaches

Bermuda has many gorgeous beaches, most tinged a delicate pink by fragments of red coral that have been eroded by water. But only 20 percent of them are open to the public. Along the South Shore there are 23 separate beaches linked by walkways in the dunes. Here is a list of the best—both public and private—in mostly west-to-east order:

Horseshoe Bay (South Shore: Southampton Parish). As the name suggests, a horseshoe-shaped bay of pink sand, popular and picturesque.

Jobson Cove (South Shore: Warwick Parish). A small beach protected by rocks and beloved by those seeking a little privacy.

Warwick Long Bay (South Shore: Warwick Parish). Ideal for a stroll along its half-mile length. The waters around the beach are also popular with windsurfers.

Elbow Beach (South Shore: Paget Parish). A long sandy stretch. Public access is along Tribe Road 4. Elbow Beach Hotel guests have direct access.

Shelly Bay (North Shore: Hamilton Parish). There are few waves here, and a gentle shelf, perfect for those learning to swim or for paddling in the shallows. Backed by soccer fields and a children's playground.

John Smith's Bay (South Shore: Smith's Parish). Two small bays with ample sand for castle building. Good for swimming and snorkeling too.

Clearwater Beach (Eastern Shore: St. George's Parish). A man-made beach lapped by crystal clear water. Scenic views across to Cooper's Island Nature Reserve.

Tobacco Bay (Bermuda's northern tip: St. George's Parish). Pretty bay with a café serving light refreshments and changing facilities for visitors.

Turn right onto Lighthouse Road to reach **Gibb's Hill Lighthouse**, which still plays an important role in protecting ships passing through the waters close to Bermuda. Built in 1846, it is one of the world's few remaining lighthouses to be constructed of iron. The light, which is now fully automated, can be seen by boats 64 km (40 miles) away. Take the 185 steps to the top for panoramic views of the island. When Britain's Queen Elizabeth II made an official visit to the lighthouse, she stopped at the roadside below to admire the view toward Riddell's Bay and the islands of Great Sound. A small bronze plaque now marks the site, designated Queen's View, where you can look at the landscape only slightly altered through the passage of time.

Gibbs Hill Lighthouse has been lighting the Bermudian coast for more than 150 years.

To the West End

One mile beyond the lighthouse, South Road joins Middle Road, which continues on toward Bermuda's West End (bus routes #7 and #8). Vestiges of the **Railway Trail** intertwine with the road in this area. Half a mile from the junction, look out for Industrial Park Road on the left, where you will find **Bermuda Brewing Company**. It produces such memorable concoctions as Wilde Hogge and Hammerhead. The brewery offers guided tours that demonstrate the brewing process from fermentation to bottling, with free samples of freshly brewed beer. In the summer months there are tours daily at 4pm; in winter the tours are on Saturday only.

Farther along Middle Road a small lane leads to West Whale Bay, a small body of water that got its name from the whales that were slaughtered here in years gone by. Port Royal Golf Course, one of the oldest on the island, fills much of this area before the road leads on to Somerset Island.

WEST END: SOMERSET AND IRELAND ISLANDS

The bridge that connects Somerset Island and its parish of Sandys (pronounced "Sands") to the main island is quite short.

Somerset Bridge, reportedly one of the world's smallest drawbridges. The original bridge dates from 1620.

The old Bermuda Railway Trail offers lovely views for the walker or cyclist.

If you travelled on immediately it would be easy to miss one of the curiosities of Bermuda, for **Somerset Bridge** is said to be the narrowest drawbridge in the world. The section which opens is wide enough to allow the passage of only a boat's mast! It is operated by simply lifting two planks of wood by hand; one has to marvel at the skill of the sailors who use the bridge regularly. The bridge and surrounding supports were renovated in 1998. The ferry service from Hamilton also stops here on its way to Dockyard. Take the ferry or walk along the old **Bermuda Railway Trail**, which is extremely scenic along this section. There are several deep "cuts" created for the rail line, with tiny wooden foot bridges over the top.

The road into **Somerset Island** leads around a pretty bay and onto **Scaur Hill Fort**, which stands on a rocky hillock hidden from the road. The fort was begun in 1869 to protect the land route to the naval dockyard at the end of the island. The layout is the so-called Prussian design, a polygon shape developed by German engineers at the time. The gunning placements held "disappearing" guns, which could not be seen from land or sea. Other gunning placements were also added by US engineers during World War II. A sturdy caponier (a small fortified room with openings for rifles) was to act as a last defense if the battlements were overrun. It was never needed, as the fort never saw any action, and today the ramparts offer panoramic views of Great Sound. There are 9 hectares (22 acres) of grassland all around the fort where you can enjoy a picnic.

Just beyond the fort, watch out for a narrow lane to the right with a sign for the **Heydon Trust Chapel**. This simple place of worship, on land set aside for personal reflection, is open at all hours for those who want to come and pray. (The building is listed on maps of 1616 as a personal residence.) Visitors can admire the architecture and see the old water storage tank that collects water for use inside.

The village of **Somerset** lies only half a mile beyond the fort. It is a small settlement but has many shops that are branches of larger Hamilton stores and also a couple of well-regarded restaurants for a leisurely lunch.

Off its far northern tip, Somerset Island is attached by bridge to a string of smaller islands: Watford Island, Boaz Island, and **Ireland Island**. It is on Ireland Island South where you will find the **Royal Naval Cemetery** set beside the main road. All navy personnel were buried here, along with many civilian

Fresh Water

There are no rivers or streams on Bermuda, and fresh water is therefore a precious resource. The earliest settlers began to collect and store rainwater, a practice that continues today. All roofs have conduits to channel rainwater into underground tanks. On older houses you may see a tank above ground, as at the chapel at Heydon Trust.

Because of the scarcity, please remember to do your part to preserve water when you visit Bermuda.

Those who gave their lives to build the Royal Naval Dockyard on Ireland Island North were buried nearby.

workers needed to run the base. A stroll along the footpath allows you to read some of the sad ends that they suffered. Sunstroke and yellow fever appear as common causes of death. So, too, does drowning from accidents in the frequent winter squalls that caught sailors unaware. Many sailors could not swim, so being lost overboard was a fate they all dreaded.

☛ The Royal Naval Dockyard

It was the Duke of Wellington who, in 1809, vowed to make Bermuda the "Gibraltar of the West" and created a plan for a massive naval base on the island. The whole project demanded far more labor than existed in the colony, so Crown prisoners were shipped here to complete the task. They were billeted in ships brought over from Britain, which were then tied up at dockside. The "hulks" (as the boats were known) were overcrowded and unsanitary. Many died from disease and malnutrition before the work was complete, but the dockyard proved to be a bastion of the British Empire and served to protect the motherland even as recently as World War II.

Postwar, the British military presence dwindled, and the main sections of the dockyard were closed in 1951. They were deserted for a number of years before being brought to life as a tourist attraction. Today, the **Royal Naval Dockyard**, on Ireland Island North, has been reborn with a number of sights and activities. You could certainly spend a morning or an afternoon exploring here.

Start your tour at the **Bermuda Maritime Museum**, opened in 1975 by Queen Elizabeth II. The museum is also home to Dolphin Quest. If traveling by bus (Routes #7 or #8), you will alight at the last stop; arriving by ferry, you should turn right from the ferry port and follow the footpath around the dock, where you will see the walls of the central fortress (or "keep") rising in front of you. The museum is entered through a large archway beyond a moat. It covers 2½ hectares (6 acres), and various collections are housed in

The Boat Loft traces the innovations of a boat-building (and boat-loving) culture.

the old brick military buildings, most of which date from the Victorian era. Where ordnance was once stored there are now collections of coins and treasure salvaged from the ocean floor. You will also find displays of diving equipment used over the centuries to explore the shipwrecks that can be found all around the treacherous reefs off the coast here.

The Boat Loft houses a collection reflecting Bermuda's innovative local designs, including a fully rigged, gleamingly polished "fitted dinghy," famed for the size of its enormous sail. Such boats were developed to allow quick access to incoming ships. In the early days, pilots were in competition with each other to reach incoming cargoes first and thus secure the business. The exhibit also details the role Bermuda has played in the world of competitive sailing. On

The Clocktower Building adds elegance to the dockyard— and some world-class shopping opportunities, too.

an island where shipbuilding was an important industry, men had the skills to design and produce fast boats. Racing started as an informal pastime, but in 1840 Samuel Triscott (a local victualer) organized the first regatta. The Bermuda Royal Yacht Club was organized in 1844 for gentlemen yachtsmen, not long after the founding of the Bermuda Native Yacht Club (BNYC) for native boatmen (many of whom were working pilots and crewmen).

After looking around these collections, climb the hill to the **Commissioner's House**, where you will find fine views of the surrounding coastline and the rest of the dockyard complex. The house, with wonderful large rooms, befits its role as home to what was once the most powerful man on the island. The whole structure is supported by an iron foundation, said to be hurricane-proof.

In the old Cooperage across the road from the Museum are the Craft Centre and the Arts Centre, both great places to search for a Bermudian souvenir. The most renowned working artists have studio spaces here, with displays of local work using such raw materials as wood, sea shells, and flowers.

Walk through the Cooperage to reach the Victualling Yard, where you will find the Tourist Information Bureau, then across the park and around the dry dock area, which is used to repair the boats and buoys so vital to ship safety. On the left is the **Bermuda Clayworks Pottery**, where you'll find experts crafting and firing ceramics with a series of island motifs.

Your walk will then lead to the **Clocktower Building**, perhaps the most elegant of the structures at dockyard. Its long lines and minimalist façade once housed administrative offices, but the interior has been transformed into a smart shopping mall with luxury goods from jewelry to cigars. Above the ground floor shops is a light, open space designed for conventions and exhibitions.

There are several restaurants in the dockyard as well as places to sit in the sunshine and have a picnic. In summer, cruise ships dock at the small port outside the main harbor wall, providing a good picture of how the working dockyard must have looked when it was home to British naval vessels.

NORTH AND EAST FROM HAMILTON

To travel north from the city of Hamilton means traversing the parishes of Pembroke, Devonshire, Smith's, and Hamilton (the latter not to be confused with the city of the same name!), then on to St. George's Parish at Bermuda's northernmost tip. The North Shore Road provides views of the rocky coastline. On the verdant South Shore there are fine period houses, many still in private hands. Two of the world's finest golf courses nestle against Harrington Sound, a large caldera now filled with tidal seawater. Finally, you reach the birthplace of this British protectorate: St. George, a picturesque town that still reflects its 17th-century beginnings.

Tiny offshore Gibbet Island (or "Gallows" Island), at the entrance to Flatts Inlet, was once the site of public hangings.

Taking Cavendish Road out of Hamilton leads to Middle Road, which runs through the widest section of land in Bermuda. Although they are never more than a mile from the sea, the people who live here are considered country dwellers by those who live on the coast.

You will come first to the **Arboretum** (bus route #3), 9 hectares (22 acres) of lawns and woods filled with native trees. Separate swaths of land concentrate on collections of ficus and palms, with an area of general woodland beyond. It's a great place for children to run wild or explore in the undergrowth.

Less than a mile past the Arboretum, you will find two churches on the right side of the road, backed by hundreds of white painted family tombs on the hillside. The larger building first catches the eye, but it is the smaller whitewashed **Old Devonshire Church** that holds the interest. The church originally erected here in 1716 was totally destroyed by a mysterious explosion on Easter Sunday, 31 March 1970. The building on the site today is an exact replica of the original and was built with money collected by public donation. The very simple interior provides the perfect environment for quiet reflection and prayer.

Old Devonshire Church went out with a bang—and came back with generous donations.

Middle Road eventually reaches the village of Flatts at the edge of **Harrington Sound**. The sound, some 3 km (2 miles) in diameter, is thought to be a huge caldera that formed after a powerful volcanic eruption. Some areas of this inland sea are immensely deep, attracting marine creatures to the safe waters. Boats also take advantage of the protective shield, and in summer (April–October) diving and snorkeling are popular pastimes. A narrow bridge fords the gap between the sound and the open sea through **Flatts Inlet**. The tidal waters are constantly flowing in and out through the 9-m (30-ft) opening. A number of boats rest on the waters of Flatts Inlet, which is one of the most photo-

*Bermudian natives (native to the surrounding sea, that is)
thrive at the Bermuda Aquarium.*

genic spots on the island. The waters have a translucent
turquoise hue that appears almost artificial, and the swaying
palms create a truly tropical scene.

On the far side of the bridge that spans the entrance to
Harrington Sound is the **Bermuda Aquarium, Natural
History Museum, and Zoo** (bus routes #3, #10, and #11).
The facilities were established in 1926 to educate visitors and
native Bermudians about life under the seas that surround
them. Over 100 species of sea creatures live in tanks, including one 145,000-gallon tank whose water is regularly
replaced by seawater from Harrington Sound. Healthy coral
reefs here support a small ecosystem. The Natural History
Museum has a number of dioramas depicting the geological
formation of the Bermudian islands and reefs, starting some

100 million years ago. It explains how the many cave systems were formed and how the hundreds of unique species of flora and fauna developed on this isolated piece of rock.

The zoo is small but extremely varied for such a small island. Important conservation work is being undertaken. The staff is working on a program to increase the numbers of flamingos in the US Virgin Islands, and you will find a small flock here successfully breeding each year. Juveniles have been sent around the world to increase the breeding stock. Golden Lion Tamarins (a South American marmoset) have also been successfully bred here. There is an interesting Australasian area, with Bennett wallabies and a *bintubong* (also called "bearcat"), a large marsupial with a prehensile tail that sits on a tree stump watching the visitors pass by.

From the Aquarium, the North Shore Road (bus routes #10 and #11) continues to the east. On the left you will find the tiny **Railway Museum**, housed in one of the old station houses. Its exhibits fascinating photographs of the railway, dubbed "the old rattle and shake" by locals. Ladies in summer hats are pictured, waiting at small platforms as the engine approaches, and trains making their way down a crowded Front Street in Hamilton. The 14 km (22 miles) of track had 44 stations along its route, but the service ran for only 16 years—from 1931 until 1947—before it accumu-

Boiling Holes

All along Bermuda's south coast, where the coral reef is close to the shore, the water has eroded columns of rock and coral whose tops lie inches below the water line. The movement of the water over and around these columns creates thousands of little bubbles, giving the impression of water boiling on the surface.

lated such heavy losses that all the rolling stock and tracks were sold to what was then British Guiana. The path of the railway line can clearly be seen in many parts of Bermuda and is now a valuable natural resource, enjoyed safely by walkers, runners, cyclists, and horse riders.

Only a couple of minutes farther along the North Shore Road is **Shelly Bay**, a picturesque sheltered beach that shelves very gently. It is backed by a park and play area, making it an ideal place to bring children. A café operates in the summer. Shelly Bay is one of the few beaches on this part of the island, which is better known for the rugged rocks running along the north shore.

> Bicycles and horse-drawn carriages creep slowly up Crawl Hill, which is really named after the corrals (or *kraals*) that once trapped fish offshore.

Bailey's Bay

Bailey's Bay is the northern section of Hamilton Parish, which you'll find just before reaching the Causeway that crosses Castle Harbour to the airport and St. George's. Bailey's Bay has a number of attractions within walking distance of each other. If traveling by bus, get off at the Swizzle Inn, famed across the island for its "Rum Swizzle" drinks (made from a secret recipe); it's also a great place for lunch.

Only a short walk west from the Inn, you will find the **Bermuda Perfumery and Gardens**. This small family business was established in 1929 by Madeleine and Herbert Scott in a garden shed. They moved to their present site in 1939 and proceeded to plant the acres of flowers that serve as raw materials to produce their small range of signature fragrances. The business has now been passed on to their son. You can take a free tour of the "factory," housed in a 200-year-old farmhouse, where you can watch the process of perfume production, including the techniques for collecting the ripe blooms. Then take your time and wander among the fragrant gardens with their swathes of jasmine, frangipani, and passion flower, their scents heavy in the warm air. You can also browse in the gift shop, which sells perfumes produced here as well as other souvenirs.

After leaving the perfumery, head back toward the Swizzle Inn and turn right at Wilkinson Avenue (by Bailey's Ice Cream Parlour). From here it is only a five-minute walk to **Crystal Caves**. The unique geological conditions that formed Bermuda created a number of cave systems. Experts claim that there are many yet to be explored and charted, and perhaps the Crystal Cave system might itself have been left undiscovered were it

*Aeons in the making: **try to make some time in your itinerary to visit the otherworldly Crystal Caves.***

not for a quirk of fate. In 1907, two young boys were playing cricket, and after a particularly good stroke they lost the ball down a small sinkhole. They decided to try to retrieve the ball and, with ropes and lanterns, they entered the hole and discovered a magical landscape 37 m (120 ft) underground. They never did find their cricket ball, but when you enter the caves you will understand why they became distracted from their original purpose. The caves have cathedral-like dimensions, with hundreds of stalactites and stalagmites hundreds of thousands of years old. The stalactites grow at a rate of 1 cm (about a half inch) every 100 years, so it is easy to begin to estimate the age of the largest structures. A clear tidal lake sits at the bottom of the cave, spanned by a pontoon bridge so you can explore the interior. Strategic lighting shows the formations to their best effect—and nature at its most awe-inspiring.

Just a short distance beyond the Swizzle Inn, near the entrance to the Grotto Bay Hotel, is the **Bermuda Glass Blowing Studio**. Here demonstrations reveal how the heat from the furnace and the skill of the glass blower combine to create beautiful and colorful objects. You can also buy one of these unusual souvenirs in the attached gallery.

The South Coast to Castle Harbour

The South Road (bus route #1) leads east from the Hamilton area, through Paget and Devonshire parishes to the southern edge of Harrington Sound and then on toward Castle Harbour. There are many large private houses here in the southeast part of the island, standing proudly behind tropical gardens. About a mile beyond the Botanical Gardens (see page 42), there is a narrow turnoff from the main road leading to **Devonshire Bay**. In summer, fishermen land their catches in the bay and sell them from small stalls set on the flat rocks surrounding the beach.

The mysteries of the glass-forming art are revealed at the Bermuda Glass Blowing Studio.

Continue your journey to the east on South Road and make a left turn at Collector's Hill, which is just before a church. Travel up the road to reach **Verdmont Museum**, a historic house on top of the hill. (There is no sign for the house from the main road.) Built on 20 hectares (50 acres) of land, Verdmont is believed to date from about 1710. Unusually, it is much more classically Georgian than Bermudian in style. It was constructed for Thomas Smith, a prominent ship owner, and several generations of his family lived here. It has a fine twelve-windowed façade—all still original—and three stories, with four rooms on each of the first two floors. The structure has remained practically unchanged and was a private home until 1951; its owners never added the modern conveniences of electricity and plumbing. Today it is brimming with

Tucker's Town has a lovely bay, though it is probably better known for the Mid Ocean Golf Club.

fine period furnishings, although only the portraits are original to the house. The wooden paneling, floors, and staircase add an elegant air to the structure. Now owned by the Bermuda National Trust, Verdmont is surrounded by a walled garden filled with herbs and fruit orchards along with a swathe of replanted forest of cedar and palmetto palms.

Farther along, South Road moves closer to the coast, and **Spittal Pond Nature Reserve** soon appears to the right. Its 14 hectares (34 acres) comprise Bermuda's largest wildlife sanctuary, a home for migratory and native bird species alike. Two ponds provide a marshy wetland, complemented by a coastal cliff environment beloved by terns and visiting longtails. Owls and the obligatory *kiskadee* inhabit the woodlands. Spittal Pond is well known for providing rest and recuperation for birds blown off course on long migratory routes: it is possible to spot unusual species that have drifted off their normal routes. Well-worn walking trails at the park are easy to follow, but be aware that there are two car parks at the sanctuary (east and west). Don't forget which one you parked in!

The main road leads east along the coast to **John Smith's Bay**, a small but much-photographed beach for swimming and snorkeling. Just beyond the bay, there is a left turn leading to **Devil's Hole Aquarium**, at the very southern tip of Harrington Sound. One of the oldest tourist attractions in Bermuda, it has been welcoming visitors since 1834. The hole is in fact a collapsed cave, producing a natural seawater aquarium that has become home to a number of voracious fish, sharks, and turtles waiting at the surface to be fed. The fish (usually large tarpon) seem to enjoy the regular food service offered by visitors. Incidentally, the name "Devil's Hole" derives from the sound of the seawater entering and leaving the hole, rather than from the fearsome reputation of some of its inhabitants.

> You needn't be an expert to explore Bermuda's caves. There are clearly marked paths and handrails, as well as guides to answer questions.

From Devil's Hole Aquarium it is possible to take the road left to the village of Flatts and the North Shore Road. However, you can go back to South Road in the direction of

The Kiskadee

Wherever you travel in Bermuda, the air will be filled with the distinct call of a unique species of bird. With its bright yellow breast, black head, and white flash above the eye, it is easily spotted. Named after its call—a clear "kis-ka-dee"—the bird was imported from Trinidad to control lizards. However, the immigrant preferred fruit and has since become a menace to local farmers.

Tucker's Town and two important golf courses. Tucker's Town is not a town but rather a collection of exclusive communities and large high-class resorts set in rolling hills and small sheltered coastal bays.

Mid Ocean Golf Course and Tucker's Point Golf Course straddle the roads here, their verdant greens and fairways tumbling across the undulating land, separated by small casuarina copses. (Be mindful of the state of play as you pass across the fairways here: there is a danger from wayward balls.) The Mid

Ocean Club is still a private members' club with a long pedigree. It has played host to many important political summits since the end of World War II, including the "Big Three" Conference in 1953 attended by Winston Churchill, Dwight D. Eisenhower, and Joseph Laniel, the French prime minister.

South Road comes to an abrupt end at Tucker's Town Bay, a small jetty and inlet with yachts bobbing gently in the water. To get across Castle Harbour to St. George's, you must go north here, taking Paynter's Road to Harrington Sound. Then

drive up along Harrington Sound Road to reach the Causeway to St. George's.

On your way up Harrington Sound Road, you will come to **Leamington Caves**, a series of caves smaller than Crystal Caves but equally spectacular. Watch also for Walsingham Lane and a sign to Tom Moore's Tavern, named after the Irish poet who spent some time on Bermuda. The tavern (which is in fact a restaurant with classic French cuisine) is open only in the evening. In the daytime you can visit **Idwal Hughes Nature Reserve**,

Not beguiled by golf? Wait out the game on any lovely beach along South Road.

also along Walsingham Lane—a pristine area of natural habitat. Collapsed limestone caves and tidal seawater mangrove swamps provide a perfect home for herons, tropical frogs, and many species of fish.

EAST END: ST. GEORGE'S AND ST. DAVID'S ISLANDS

To reach the remaining portions of Bermuda, including the airport and St. George's town, you must take the narrow **Causeway** across Castle Harbour. The concrete Causeway was built as a temporary substitute for the bridge lost after a hurricane in the early part of the 20th century, but it has never been replaced. If you travel by motorcycle on a windy day, be sure to take extra care as the gusts can be quite strong. There is a small swing-bridge at the far end that can be slippery when wet; however, the middle lanes have been created specially for the passage of mopeds and bicycles.

Until a bridge was first built in 1934, residents of St. David's Island could reach St. George's only by ferry.

Once over the Causeway, you are on St. David's Island. You'll see the airport terminal immediately ahead. The road travels between the airport and runway on the right and the turquoise waters of Ferry Reach on the left. A large white building houses the **Bermuda Biological Station for Research**, established in 1903 to perform marine studies in conjunction with Harvard University and the Bermuda Natural History Society. A traffic circle (roundabout) past the airport leads left to St. George's and right to St. David's.

St. David's Island

Now larger in area than St. George's Island, **St. David's Island** was one of the most isolated of the populated islands that make up Bermuda until 1940, when the British government leased the area to the US military. The island was needed as a military base but was too small for that purpose, so extra land was reclaimed from the sea to create a land area big enough for an air base and naval station. Much of St. David's subsequently became a small piece of the US on British soil. Activity has slowly been wound down in recent years, and US service personnel are not as numerous as during the post-World War II years.

To reach St. David's town, travel along St. David's Road from the traffic circle on the far side of the airport. (Bus route #6 travels to St. David's from St. George's.) The native population of St. David's has always been noted for

St. David's Lightouse offers a perfect vantage point for viewing migrating whales.

its fishing skills. The original town grew up around the British military batteries built to protect the southern entrance to St. George's Harbour. The town is still in the protection business, but today it looks out for the shipping that passes through the waters around Bermuda.

King's Square in St. Georges Town, where once foodstuffs were sold and criminals were punished.

St. David's Lighthouse stands on the highest point on the eastern tip of the island and sends its beam 32 km (20 miles) over the ocean. The structure took three years to build, and the light was activated on 3 November 1879. It also acts as the finishing line for such major yacht races as the Newport-Bermuda. Groups of humpbacked whales that pass through Bermuda waters in April and May can clearly be seen from this vantage point.

Off the coast to the south of St. David's Island is smaller **Nonsuch Island**, once a quarantine station for sufferers of yellow fever. In 1951, a small colony of Bermuda petrels was discovered to be nesting on Nonsuch, and it has remained a sanctuary for the birds since that time. Visits are limited but can be made by arrangement with Bermuda Biological Station for Research (Tel: 297-1880).

St. George's Island

Back at the airport, cross the bridge and turn left to get to Ferry Point, an important strategic area of land at the western tip of St. George's Island. There are no less than three separate fortifications here protecting the entrance to St. George's Harbour. The earliest was Burnt Point Fort, built in 1688 to help stop illegal trading by local sailors. The Ferry Island Fort, on a small island a short distance offshore, was begun in the 1790s and was almost constantly developed for the next 80 years. In 1823, Major Thomas Blanchard constructed Martello Tower on high ground behind the two forts, where soldiers could survey the surrounding land and coastline. Today the remains of all three fortifications comprise **Ferry Point Park**, where it is possible to explore the

The Bermuda Triangle

In the centuries of exploration after Columbus and his fellow explorers began to chart the seas, Bermuda gained a reputation as an "island of devils." This was attributed in the early years to the treacherous reefs that could destroy ships. The 20th century witnessed a series of new mysteries, which still fascinate mankind today.

Stories abound of an area of sea where ships vanish or are found without a crew. Squadrons of planes have also disappeared. This fearful place has become known as the "Bermuda Triangle" because the island is at its northern point.

Alien abduction and anomalies in the earth's magnetic field are two of the theories that have been proposed for such happenings. Although there is as yet no plausible explanation for the mysteries, experts tell us that the Bermuda Triangle is in fact no more dangerous than many other tracks of sea. Yet we all still enjoy the frisson of excitement of the unknown.

forts at your leisure, walk through woodland, and enjoy the beauties of Lover's Lake. It is a wonderful place to have a picnic, and it's relatively quiet, even on a summer weekend.

Returning to Ferry Point junction, take the north fork to St. George's town. You'll travel around the far side of Mullet Bay —a sheltered natural harbor for small craft—and then past a children's play area before reaching the outskirts of town. (St. George's can be reached via bus routes #1, #3, #10, and #11.) Set in the far northeast portion of Bermuda, St. George's, a UNESCO World Heritage Site since 2000, is the island's oldest town and the historic heartland of the colony. Sir George Somers and his brave band of settlers were heading for Virginia in 1609 when they were shipwrecked on reefs just offshore from here. They were surprised by the natural riches that Bermuda had to offer, as the island had good cedar wood to build more ships. Out of adversity came good fortune, and the settlers soon built two new ships and sailed from Bermuda to complete their original goal of reaching Jamestown. Somers returned to Bermuda the following year but died here before he could develop the town further.

The settlers who founded the town in 1615 created a basic grid pattern that has remained unchanged. The lanes in town are wide enough for a horse and carriage, but no wider. They retain their original names, some with reference to local characters and activities such as Printer's Alley and Aunt Peggy's Lane. Main streets such as Queen Street and Duke of York Street recall the monarchs and individuals important to the British Crown. Take time to wander along the narrow lanes —beyond the noise of contemporary Bermuda—where you can imagine yourself back in the 16th and 17th centuries. The town is small, so it is difficult to lose your way. As you walk, you will find many historic houses and museums providing many more clues to the lives of these fascinating people.

Start at **King's Square** on the waterfront. Originally known as "Market Square," it was the center of all activity for the town. Here you will find the Visitors' Service Bureau, whose helpful staff will be able to supply you with information about the day's activities. On the east side of the square is the **Town Hall**, which dates from 1782. Although relatively young by St. George's standards, it has wonderful cedar wood floors and ceilings. Here you can find out about the previous lord mayors and view a commemorative "Charles and Diana" signature, harkening back to happy times.

At the northwest corner of the square is the **Bermuda Museum of the National Trust**. This 17th-century building was constructed by Governor Samuel Day, who arrived from England, found the old governor's house in disrepair, and built this house using government land and government wood— yet he refused to hand over the house when he was ousted from office after only two years. The house became a hotel, the Globe, in the mid-19th century but attracted notoriety again in the early 1860s when it became the office of a Confederate agent during the US Civil War. In 1952, the house was acquired by the Bermuda Historical Monuments Trust and was opened as a museum in 1961, with substantial refurbishment in 1996.

Vestiges of St. George's Town's British heritage decorate its Town Hall.

On the ground floor, pride of place is given to a detailed model of Somers's ship, *Sea Venture*. Many American visitors are also fascinated by a replica of a machine commissioned by the Congress of the Confederate States that stamped a seal for all their official documents. There is also a short video presentation called "Bermuda: Centre of the Atlantic," which tells the story of the founding and development of the island. Climb the stairs to the first floor, where the so-called Rogues and Runners Museum presents a detailed exposition of Bermuda's role in the American Civil War. Bermuda had many ties with the southern states through both business and family bloodlines. Although Britain officially remained neutral, Bermudians favored the South, wanting to help their friends—and make a lot of money in the process. A series of short information boards brings to life different aspects of this intriguing time in Bermuda's history. Sadly, it also documents the true story of the blockade-runner *Fannie,* which returned from one trip in June 1864 with two sick crew members. The yellow fever they carried soon spread across Bermuda, killing many hundreds of people. Graves in the Royal Naval Cemetery (near the dockyard at the other end of Bermuda) offer testimony to some of the individuals who succumbed to this dreadful disease.

Another of Bermuda's irresistible photo opportunities: have your picture taken "imprisoned" in the stocks at King's Square.

In King's Square, you can witness re-enactments of many of its historic functions. The town crier will call the news of the day, and wrongdoers will be punished in the stocks that sit outside the Bank of Butterfield building. Nearby on the water's edge is a dunking stool, used in times past for nagging wives or busybodies. Today, local ladies dressed in costume brave the waters to the delight of visitors.

A small bridge leads to **Ordnance Island**, a tiny island only 9 m (30 ft) offshore, used today as a cruise dock in summer months. Named for the guns once kept there, it was used also to hang condemned prisoners. Today it has two important monuments dating back to the birth of the British colony of Bermuda. On the left is a full-size replica of the ship *Deliverance,* one of two vessels that Sir George Somers and his group of settlers rebuilt following the shipwreck of the *Sea Venture* in 1609. The tiny interior is not for the claustrophobic and gives a good idea of how difficult the journey must have been, as the passengers

Sir George is memorialized in the town that everyone calls his own.

huddled together in a minuscule, poorly ventilated space with only rudimentary sanitation. To the right of the bridge to Ordnance Island is a sculpture of Somers by a leading Bermudian artist, Desmond Fountain. It depicts a wind- and sea-swept Sir George in a dramatic—perhaps anguished—pose with arms outstretched.

In the town around King's Square are a delightful number of attractions that tell the story of St. George's from the early 17th-century settlement to the changes that have taken place in modern times. To the left of Town Hall is a walkway lead-

The Tucker House Museum preserves the antique accouterments of a leading Bermudian dynasty.

ing to King Street (a cobbled road) and two important historical buildings. The first is **Bridge House**, an L-shaped building on the left side. This is the oldest inhabited structure on the island (dating from about 1700) and is still in remarkably good condition considering the volatile weather that it has undoubtedly had to contend with. It is named Bridge House because it sat opposite a small wooden bridge that once led to the harbor here. The house, now owned by the National Trust of Bermuda, is split into apartments that can be visited on certain days each year (details are available from the National Trust). However, part of the building also houses the Bridge House Gallery, a commercial gallery selling Bermudian art. The original design of the building can clearly be seen in the interior of the gallery. Many of the earliest Governors of Bermuda lived here, including Alured

Popple, famed for his statesmanly handling of the island's affairs and the reinforcing of her defenses.

At the top of King Street is **State House**, built in the 1620s to house Bermuda's Assembly. Today it is the oldest stone building on the island. The plain façade and sturdy walls were designed to withstand hurricanes and the worst of the summer humidity. It was used continuously until 1815, when the island's capital was moved from St. George's to Hamilton. The local Masonic lodge negotiated with the Assembly to use the building, with a rent of one peppercorn per year, a price that remains in force to this day. The "peppercorn" rent is handed over to the crown in one of the most ornate ceremonial occasions of the year, with the mayor and town officials in full official regalia.

Water Street leads away from King's Square to the west. It has many shops selling tax-free goods; the modern shops occupy space in much older buildings. Wander along the traffic-free thoroughfare to do some leisurely souvenir hunting. On your right, watch for **Tucker House Museum**, which was from 1775 the home of Henry Tucker, the

Klinker-Built

The distinctive roofs of Bermuda's houses have an unusual story. The original settlers knew little about architecture and had problems building a roof that could withstand the sometimes fierce winter storms of the Atlantic. After several abortive designs, they hit upon the idea of using their skills as ship builders to solve the problem. The roofs were simply built like upside-down ship hulls, one layer of limestone overlapping another, just as wooden planks are laid on a ship's hull. The design was a remarkable success and has been used on houses ever since.

President of the Governor's Council. The Tuckers were one of the most influential families on Bermuda, the first family member having arrived on the island in 1616. In 1950, a descendant—an American named Robert Tucker—bequeathed many family heirlooms to the house in his will. The kitchen area, originally separated from the main house, was once a barbershop operated by Henry Raine, a black man who came to Bermuda to escape the worst of the American Civil War. Once the war was over, he and his family returned to the US, where he became the first black member elected to the House of Representatives.

Across the street is the **Carriage Museum**. Until the 1940s, horses and carriages were the only modes of transportation permitted along the narrow Bermuda roads, and almost every well-to-do family had a horse-drawn vehicle. How-

> **Friendly Bermudians welcome visitors to meetings of such organizations as the Rotary Club, Bridge Club, Croquet Club, and the English Speaking Union.**

ever, these disappeared almost immediately following a relaxation of the strict rules that had kept motor vehicles off the island. This collection of beautiful carriages celebrates those "gone-but-not-forgotten" days.

 St. Peter's Church sits on Duke of York Street, now the main route through the town. Originally built in 1612, it is the oldest Anglican church in the Western Hemisphere still regularly used for services; much of the present structure dates from 1713. The beautiful building is filled with Bermudian cedar for the roof supports and the pews. The font is even older than the church itself and was brought with the earliest settlers from a previous church in England. Pride of place goes to the collection of silver, the chalice, the chalice set, and the alms basin, all dating from the 17th century.

The church has also kept old coins dating from 1616. Behind the south churchyard you can find the Old Rectory, built in the 18th century for pirate George Drew and kept in beautiful order by the Bermuda National Trust.

Take Duke of Kent Street north from the town center to reach a number of important attractions. Almost immediately on the left is **St. George's Historical Society Museum**, set in an 18th-century house that was once home to the Mitchell family. Walk up the "welcome arms" staircase (a common feature of family homes of the era) and step into a treasure-trove of Bermudiana. Furniture, clothing, and works of art have all been donated or bought to add to the

St. George's Historical Society Museum offers a taste of Bermudian life—and of Bermudian banana bread.

The Unfinished Church, a ruin that never was a building, is a striking sight even in its strange condition.

fascinating—and constantly growing—collection. Here is everything from buttons to bottles to old bathtubs. The kitchen at the back of the house is filled with authentic pieces: earthenware jars for storage, copper cups for measuring, iron pots for cooking. The admission price includes tea and Bermudian banana bread.

Around the corner in Featherbed Alley, you will find **Featherbed Alley Printery**, a small museum with a working model of the Gutenberg printing press first brought from England by Joseph Stockdale in 1783 and used to produce the *Bermuda Gazette*—first issued on 17 January 1784. The building where the paper was originally printed is the Stockdale House, on the corner of Printer's Alley and Needle and Thread Alley. Stockdale was an extremely industrious man and also a man of foresight, as he also organized and ran the first postal service on the island.

Continue along Duke of Kent Street and you will come to the **Unfinished Church**, an elegant edifice originally begun in the 1870s when St. Peter's Church was badly damaged by a storm and thought to be beyond repair. As construction proceeded, however, the local population decided that they would rather invest their money in repairing the old church and work on the unfinished church was immediately stopped. Had the church been completed, it would have been a fitting place of worship.

Continue to the right of the Unfinished Church, up Government Hill Road and through the rolling fairways of St. George's Golf Course, one of the most challenging on the island, until you reach the coast. Here you will find **Tobacco Bay**, a small stretch of sheltered beach popular with the cruise passengers who disembark at St. George's and want to spend time sunbathing. It was here in 1775 that 100 barrels of gunpowder mysteriously disappeared from stores in Fort St. Catherine and found their way onto a boat bound for the use of the American revolutionaries.

Drive past the sheltered inlet of Coot Pond to reach **Fort St. Catherine** itself. (Or you can take a minibus, which runs from King's Square to the fort every 15 minutes.) The setting of the fort—on a rocky promontory with sandy beaches on both flanks—is spectacular, with strong walls rising on all sides. The fort was begun as early as 1614 but has been upgraded throughout Bermuda's history. Major renovations took place in 1793, 1820, and 1840 as technology improved and weaponry developed. The last major upgrade was completed in 1878.

Explore the outer walls and impressive battlements before visiting the exhibitions housed in the interior. Collections of antique weapons, including swords and muskets, outline the progress made in weapons technology. Replicas of the crown jewels housed in the Tower of London can also be found here. An audiovisual presentation gives a comprehensive overview of all the fortifications on Bermuda.

There are two other small fortifications to the south of Fort St. Catherine. Alexandra Battery lies halfway along Barry Road, and the tiny **Gates Fort** sits at the mouth of Town Cut, the navigation route for boats entering St. George's Harbour. Gates Fort first appeared on maps as "Danver's Fort" in 1626. It became obsolete in the 19th century and was used as a family home from 1870 until 1922 before being restored by the government. The site, once used to stop suspect and enemy boats from entering the harbor, is now a great place to welcome the large cruise vessels making their way into Bermuda. Town Cut is only a few hundred feet across; ships dwarf the surrounding islands and appear to pass through with only inches on either side. One wonders what the old defenders of Gates Fort would have felt about these huge vessels looming upon them. It is a truly exhilarating sight.

Moon Gates

A number of narrow limestone arches—locally called "moon gates"—can be found across Bermuda. They have been borrowed from the Chinese gates said to bring luck to those who walk through them. Moon gates are particularly lucky for lovers, who should make a wish as they walk through in unison. They are, therefore, a particularly popular venue for weddings, where bride and groom finish the ceremony by passing under the gate and making a wish for their new life together.

WHAT TO DO

We provide local Bermuda phone numbers for many of the activities mentioned in this chapter. When calling from outside the islands, remember to dial Bermuda's own area code (441) before the seven-digit number.

RECREATION AND SPORTS

Bermuda is an ideal vacation destination for outdoor activities. Summer brings warm (but not hot) weather and warm sea temperatures, making it ideal for diving, snorkeling, and other water sports. On land, you can fill your day with tennis and golf along with long walks and beach activities. In winter, the sea temperature makes it a little too cold for diving, but many visitors still enjoy swimming in waters warmer than at home, and all land activities are thoroughly enjoyable with the addition of a jacket or sweater. The Bermuda Tourist Board produces *Bermuda—What to Do,* a comprehensive brochure with contact information and prices on a range of sporting activities.

Love the links? There are almost too many courses to choose from here.

Golf

Bermuda is known as a golfer's paradise and has a greater concentration of courses than in any other country in the world. It's not only the quantity that makes Bermuda great but also the quality of the courses, many created by the best designers in the world. The greens and fairways are kept in pristine condition. The courses are challenging, and the hills and coastline also help to create links reminiscent of those in Scotland—but with much better weather.

A couple of Bermuda's championship courses are world famous, but all are engrossing. Several hotels have courses on their own grounds, but all hotels and guesthouses can arrange an introduction to the club you'd like to play. Be sure to have them phone ahead to set the starting time. Here is a brief survey of clubs, from west to east:

Port Royal Golf Course (Southampton Parish): 6,561 yards, par 71. Government-owned and open to the public, this Robert Trent Jones course dates from 1970. A couple of fairways cling to clifftops over the Atlantic, adding thrills to some impressively serious golf.

Fairmont Southampton Princess Golf Club (Southampton Parish): 2,737 yards, par 54 executive course. The Gibb's Hill lighthouse overhead is only one of the sights on this 18-hole par-three course.

Riddell's Bay Golf and Country Club (Warwick Parish): 5,713 yards, par 70. Hilly and windy, with narrow fairways. The first hole, at 418 yards, par four, is Bermuda's toughest starter.

Belmont Golf Club (Warwick Parish): 5,759 yards, par 70. All very challenging, with tight fairways, elevated greens, blind second shots, and headwinds on steep headlands.

The Mid Ocean Club's stunning beauty distracts many a golfer who attempts its seriously challenging course.

Ocean View Golf and Country Club (Devonshire Parish): nine holes, 2,940 yards, par 35. Government-owned and open to the public. Ocean View is right in the center of the Main Island and overlooks the north coast.

Mid Ocean Club (Tucker's Town): 6,512 yards, par 71. The name is often mentioned when the pros discuss the greatest golf courses in the world. With its big greens and awesome obstacles, this is Bermuda's longest and most thrillingly beautiful course. Home run king Babe Ruth couldn't clear Mangrove Lake, the big wet problem on the 5th hole; he lost 11 balls.

Tucker's Point Golf Club (Hamilton Parish): 6,361 yards, par 70. The course (formerly Castle Harbour) was originally designed by Robert Trent Jones. It has been completely

Perfect weather, a view to die for, and championship-quality golf courses: you really couldn't ask for more.

revamped and refurbished. From the elevated first tee, the panorama of green land, blue-green harbor, and dark blue sea stirs the heart. At only 312 yards, this par four starts the day with confidence, but beautiful complications quickly follow.

St. George's Golf Club (St. George's Parish): 4,043 yards, par 62. Located on the eastern tip of the island, the course adjoins the St. George's Club Village, overlooking Fort St. Catherine.

Walking

The old Railway Trail is Bermuda's premier walkway, with miles of safe paths through the heart of the island and along some of its prettiest stretches of coastline. The Bermuda

Department of Tourism has issued a booklet guide for visitors, with maps showing the main features of the route.

Another area for safe and picturesque walking is along the sand dunes behind the South Shore beaches. These link the main public beaches (from Warwick Long Bay to Horseshoe Bay). They also provide access to secret coves. Park in any of the beach parking lots along the south coast to reach the paths.

For a personal touch, there are a number of guides who provide guided walks full of interesting details of local history. Contact Bermuda Lectures and Tours (Tel: 234-4082; fax: 238-2773) for further details or to arrange a custom itinerary.

Water Sports

With many shallow lagoons, Bermuda is a great place for windsurfing, jet skiing, pedalos, or aquacycling. Most large hotels will have some equipment for hire. If they don't have what you need, contact Blue Water Diver and Watersports,

> **Be polite. In shops, Bermudians stand in orderly lines and greet one another courteously, saying "Please," "Thank you," and "Excuse me."**

which has comprehensive facilities at three sites: Somerset Bridge, Elbow Beach, and the Newstead Hotel. You can reach them at P.O. Box SN 165, Southampton, SN BX, Bermuda; Tel: 234-1034/2909/2911 fax: 232-3670; website <www.divebermuda.com>.

Parasailing is also available, but please make sure that you are fully insured before taking to the air. Many policies exclude this popular activity.

Diving and Snorkeling

The diving and snorkeling opportunities in Bermuda are many and varied. The water temperature ranges from 17°C

(62°F) in winter to a warm 28°C (83°F) in summer. The clear waters in the western Atlantic, with numerous reefs and rocky outcrops, offer an ideal habitat for many hundreds of species of fish along with healthy coral for parrot fish, angel fish, and huge, gentle groupers. Deeper water supports such creatures as sharks, turtles, and dolphins.

The shallow bays and rocky inlets around the coast are ideal snorkeling territory. Visibility can reach about 60 m (nearly 200 ft) since there is very little water pollution here and the reefs offer protection against the rolling waves of the outer ocean. Most hotels will have snorkeling equipment that you can rent to explore close to shore. If you want to snorkel out in the large shallow reefs on the northern side of the island, there are a number of companies offering morning or full-day trips with equipment included. One is Barefoot Cruises (Tel: 236-3498); another is Jessie James Cruises (Tel: 296-5801).

Bermuda's reefs provide excellent dive sites either in the shallows or on the ocean side walls that drop steeply into the colder, deeper water. The ships that have foundered on reefs in the waters off Bermuda have left over 365 wrecks to explore. Even the scant remains of the *Sea Venture* (which sank in 1609) can be located and identified. Others are far more exciting for divers, including Harrington Sound, the South Shore reef wall, and the wreck of the *Vixen* (just off Somerset Long Bay on Somerset Island).

There are a number of dive centers that provide transport to the sites and experienced and qualified dive masters to assist. Fantasea Bermuda offers diving instruction and accompanied dives as well as introductory sessions. It operates from two locations, Albuoys Point (Tel: 236-1300, fax: 236-

All manner of sea creatures populate Bermuda's reefs and wrecks, making for an unforgettable snorkeling experience.

0926) and Sonesta Beach Resort (Tel: 238-1833, fax: 236-0394); website <www.fantasea.bm>). In addition, Nautilus Diving offers instruction and introductory sessions (Tel: 295-9485; fax: 234-5180; website <www.bermuda.bm/nautilus>). Remember to bring your dive certificate, as you will be allowed to rent equipment and dive only if you can prove your competence.

If you wish to learn to dive in Bermuda, there are a number of dive centers that offer training to professional levels. All are affiliated with one of the major certifying bodies, with PADI (Professional Association of Diving Instructors) being the most common. The basic qualification—the Open Water Certificate—takes five days to complete. This will allow you to dive with an instructor to a depth of 18 m (60 ft), which opens many dive sites in Bermuda to you. Blue Water Divers and Watersports offers a certification program. They have three locations around the island (see page 85; Tel: 234-1034; website <www.divebermuda.com>).

For those who would like to experience the underwater environment at first hand but don't want to dive or can't swim, there are two companies that operate a "helmet diving" system. Walk on the sandy sea bottom only 2½ m (8 ft) under the surface wearing a helmet that supplies a constant supply of oxygen. Here you can explore shallow reefs and watch the marine life swim right by. All tours are supervised by guides. Greg Hartley's Under Sea Adventures operates from Watford Bridge Ferry Dock in Somerset daily at 10am and 1:30pm (Tel: 234-2861). Bermuda Bell Diving is located in Flatts Village (Tel: 292-4434; fax: 295-7235).

Fishing and Sport Fishing

The waters around the island are teeming with fish all year round. This is especially true during the summer months,

Even if they aren't biting—which doesn't happen very often—a day on a boat in Bermuda is not a day wasted.

when Bermuda is on the path of many migratory species. Sport fishing is hugely popular and can be arranged at a number of sites around the island. The local guides are especially experienced and helpful.

The deepwater sounds are where the big fish such as marlin, sailfish, barracuda, and tuna run. These can be found all around the outer reef, but expert local help is needed to pinpoint the best spots, weather, water conditions, and times of year for each fish species. Reef fishing by boat offers the opportunity to catch amberjack, snapper, and chub. Fishing from the coastline beaches and docks can be just as exciting, with bonefish, barracuda for sport, and snapper for eating.

Sport fishing boats can be rented at most major marinas. Prices vary, but a full day's rental of boat and crew would be between $400 and $500. Half-day rentals are also available.

If you haven't seen enough sea life while fishing and diving, you can always get up close at Dolphin Quest.

Russell Young aboard *Sea Wolfe* offers private or split trips sailing from Somerset (Tel: 234-1832; fax: 234-2930; website <www.sportfishbermuda.com>). Eureka Fishing Ltd. has a large-party fishing boat, with per-person rates (Tel: 297-2252; fax: 295-3620; website <www.bermudashorts.bm/eureka>).

Sailboat Tours

If you don't sail yourself, this is a great way to see Bermuda from the water, including the many small islands lying just off

Hamilton Harbour and St. George's Harbour. Wind Sail Charters has various cruises (Tel: 238-0825).

Spectator Sports

Bermudians are a particularly sociable yet competitive people who take enthusiastically to sports. There are many important sporting leagues and clubs whose competitions bring out the whole community.

The game of cricket is Bermuda's life blood, and the Cup Match is the premier sporting—and social —event of the year. The whole island is in a holiday mood when the event is held in late July or early August, and most shops and many restaurants close. Everyone's attention focuses on enjoying the day. You are not just watching the match; you are watching a society at play.

Bermuda's maritime heritage can be seen most clearly in the many regattas and ocean races held during the summer. Local Bermuda dinghies, with white sails unfurled, cut through the azure waters. Large sleek sailboats ply the Atlantic from the US in an ocean-going race at least once each year, and there is nothing quite like watching these beautiful vessels arrive in harbor (see page 95). Large crowds gather in Hamilton to welcome winner and losers alike.

There are also frequent golf, tennis, and rugby tournaments. Road races, carting, fun runs, triathlons, and marathons are all regular activities, and many of Bermuda's sporting associations hold invitationals or open tournaments. If you have a special sporting interest, it would be worthwhile contacting the Bermuda Department of Tourism for specific information.

ENTERTAINMENT

Hotels and resorts will of course have regular shows and performances in their facilities, some quite spectacular. Nightlife outside the hotel and resort scene is concentrated in cafés, clubs, and pubs in the main towns.

Break in those dancing shoes and listen to local beats in a Hamilton nightclub.

Nightclubs and discos are mainly in Hamilton.

Local clubs and stage shows reflect such Bermudian and Caribbean traditions as steelband music, calypso, goombay, reggae, and limbo dancing, among others. There is also a thriving local rock 'n' roll scene.

In the winter season (November through March), nightlife can be much quieter. But the annual Bermuda Arts Festival takes up the slack starting in January with a series of concerts, opera, plays, art exhibits, and other cultural events featuring performers and artists from around the world. The Festival is extremely popular with native Bermudians, which means many performances sell out immediately. The Tourist Office has information, or you can contact Bermuda Festival Ltd. (Tel: 295-1291; fax: 295-7403; website <www.bermudafestival.com>).

Watching Ceremonies

Bermuda has a full series of ceremonial activities throughout the summer months, all based on the traditions of British "pomp and circumstance." Such events as the Opening of Parliament, the Beat Retreat Ceremony, and the "Peppercorn" Ceremony are colorful, exciting, and rich in history. They also bring out the whole community, and attending makes you feel as though you are a part of Bermudian society.

The Bermuda Regiment Band is called out on numerous ceremonial occasions throughout the year.

SHOPPING

Bermuda is not a duty-free island. In fact, since there is no income tax for the local population, charging duty on imported goods is one way for the government to raise funds. Duty varies on the type of goods but is always included in the price. However, there is no sales tax at all in Bermuda, so here is your opportunity to save a little.

Tax-free shops will claim to save you up to 30 percent on prices back home, but this is not universal. It is always important to do some research at home before you arrive so that you can compare prices. Some goods are only a little cheaper in Bermuda, but you might want a "real" bargain.

In many ways, Bermuda is still a vendor of fine British goods, although the range of merchandise is definitely expanding. Bermudian traders have always bought directly from the manufacturers rather than through middlemen, which has traditionally resulted in a cheaper price than you would find at home. However, government-imposed import duty means that prices might not be as advantageous as they once were. The key to tax-free shopping in Bermuda today is quality, not price.

There is a comprehensive range of quality luxury goods on sale in the major towns on the island. Front Street in Hamilton is a shopper's delight, and the staff offer a helpful and not overpowering sales service. You can browse here in a relaxed, unpressured atmosphere.

The best in crystal, porcelain tableware, silver cutlery, and jewelry can be found, and savings can be made by discerning shoppers on such names as Waterford, Wedgwood, Baccarat, and Royal Doulton. Other popular imports from the British Isles include Scottish and Irish tweed, cashmere, and genuine tartans.

The oldest department store is Trimingham's, which has a comprehensive range of designer goods such as perfume and clothing,

Calendar of Events

There are many events in Bermuda; it would be impossible to note every one. Below are some of the highlights. For a detailed listing, check the website: <www.bermudatourism.com>.

January–March	Bermuda Arts Festival (see page 92).
February	Bermuda Horse and Pony Assoc. Show.
March	Bermuda All-Breed Championship Dog Show and Cat Fanciers Show; Regimental Music Display.
April	Peppercorn Ceremony when the old Masonic Lodge of Bermuda pays its rent.
May–October	Beat Retreat Ceremony, alternating between Hamilton St. Georges and Royal Naval Dockyard (excluding August).
May	Bermuda Grand Art Festival by the Sea; Bermuda International Film Festival; Daytona–Bermuda Yacht Race (odd years only).
June	Queen's Birthday (public holiday); Bermuda Ocean Race (even years only); Marion–Bermuda Cruising Yacht Race (odd years only).
July–October	Heritage Nights in St. George's: late-night shopping, with craft and food stalls (Tuesday evenings).
late July/ early August	Cup Match (cricket tournament played since 1902).
September	Bermuda Mixed Foursomes Amateur Golf Championship; Bank of Bermuda Triathlon week.
October	National Match Sailing Championship; King Edward VII Gold Cup, match sailing.
November	Opening of Parliament; Bermuda Tattoo; Bermuda Lawn Tennis Invitational; Remembrance Day (public holiday).
December	St. George's New Year's Eve Celebration.

The Royal Naval Dockyard, with its shopping mall and Arts Centre, should satisfy even the most ardent shopoholic.

but other stores act as exclusive agents for certain producers (for example, Bluck's and Cooper's specialize in china and crystal).

Bermuda's shops sell gold and silver jewelry and gemstones such as diamonds, sapphires, and emeralds set in gold. There are also unusual and rare gold and silver coins recovered from treasures found on the seabed and mounted in gold to be worn as pendants or brooches. A comprehensive range of watches by names such as Rolex, Breitling, and Tag Heuer are also available, along with fragrances from around the world.

Art and Handicrafts

Painting. Several artists create watercolor images of Bermuda, and their bright harbor scenes or elegant details of cottages will bring back many happy memories of your trip. Michael Swan depicts Bermudian architecture in minimalist fashion, while artists such as Carole Holding or Bruce Stuart paint a more literal picture. Ronnie Chameau is an artist who works with watercolor, clay, and dried grass to create a range of beautiful art. She has a shop in the Trimingham store in Hamilton.

Sculpture. Desmond Fountain is a Bermudian sculptor whose work can be seen all over the island. The impression of Sir George Somers on Ordnance Island in St. George's is his most noted work, but he also accepts commissions to produce beautiful life-sized models and smaller pieces. He has a gallery at 69 Front Street, Hamilton.

Galleries. Visit the Arts Centre at the Royal Naval Dockyard to view a range of styles. In St. George's, the Bridge House Art Gallery and Craft Shop (on King Street) has a range of work and represents over 25 artists. Windjammer Gallery (on King Street in Hamilton) has a comprehensive selection of pieces by local artists.

Woodwork. Bermudian cedar has been used to construct and decorate homes, churches, and public buildings for over 300 years and makes a fitting souvenir. Able wood turners now create bowls and carvings that bring out the beauty of the grain. Since cedar is now rare, other woods are also used.

Ceramics. The Bermuda Clayworks Pottery (at the Royal Naval Dockyard) produces a number of patterns, several with island themes.

Glass. The Bermuda Glass Blowing Studio (at Bailey's Bay) melds the skill of the glassblower and the heat of the furnace to produce a range of articles such as plates, small animals, and beautiful Christmas decorations.

Clothing

If you don't feel like packing for Bermuda, take an empty bag and buy your holiday wardrobe when you arrive in the islands.

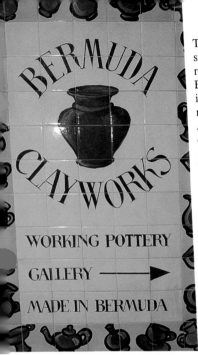

WORKING POTTERY

GALLERY ───────▶

MADE IN BERMUDA

Watch Bermudian ceramics being made — and find the perfect piece to take home.

The Front Street department stores in Hamilton have a full range of fashion items from Europe, and there are many independent boutiques with ready-to-wear collections. And as in any other tourist destination, there are plenty of shops selling beachwear and T-shirts galore.

Collectibles

The sea has played an important role in the history of Bermuda, and there is a range of nautical-themed items to purchase. Propellers, brass plates, and displays of nautical knots will remind you of the regatta or ocean yacht race.

The military and colonial legacy of Bermuda, plus a natural tendency for most Bermudian families in the past never to throw anything away, means that the island is a treasure trove of collectibles. Many items found their way over from Britain, so old tins, buttons, bottles, and items of china and brass are numerous. You'll find small stalls and shops in the alleys of Hamilton and on the roadside as you travel around the island where you can lose yourself for hours searching for that little piece of the past to take home with you.

Food

The mild climate and abundant fruit help to produce some interesting and tasty foodstuffs to take home. Bermuda honey has a distinctive taste and is sold at many small roadside vegetable stalls. Marmalade and preserves have been made for centuries to prolong food supplies for the islanders, and you can choose from a wide range of flavors.

Alcohol and Liquor

Dealing in alcohol and liquor is one of the longest-standing trades in Bermuda, and you will find the finest products from around the world. However, alcohol is duty-free only if bought to take off the island, not when purchased for consumption on the island. You will not be allowed to take these purchases with you when you leave the store, but they will be delivered to the airport for you to collect just before you leave Bermuda.

> Feel free to dress well in Bermuda, where local residents enjoy the formalities of social and dining occasions.

Prices for brands that you have at home might not be cheaper than at your local store, so please undertake some research before you leave for your trip.

ACTIVITIES FOR CHILDREN

There's nothing that young visitors like better than a sandy beach and the sea; they can play for hours in the shallows or build sandcastles on the shore. Most of the major resorts have clean, safe beaches with good facilities.

Always remember to cover youngsters' skin with a suitable sunscreen and to limit their time in the sun for the first few days: Bermuda has very clear air, resulting in more of the damaging rays reaching the surface. Also make sure they are well supervised whenever they are near the water.

Some large hotel complexes will offer special programs for children. Some might even have a special club where children can make new friends and spend the whole day in pursuit of such activities as face painting. Also be aware that certain hotels in Bermuda have an adults-only policy or few facilities specifically for children. Always research the facilities available at any hotel before you make a reservation.

For the Young-at-Heart

Below are some attractions that are ideal for younger visitors (see page 36 for hours and locations).

Carriage rides. A horse and buggy trip is an exciting way to see Hamilton—and to be seen by everyone in town.

Ferry rides. "Landlubbers" of all ages will have fun going across Hamilton Bay, through the shallow waters, past small islands, and into the tiny harbors.

Beat Retreat Ceremony. Children are fascinated by the sound of the drums and bagpipes and by the colorful uniforms. Expect them to march all the way back to the hotel.

The *Deliverance*. Set them loose to explore this fascinating replica of the ship built by Admiral Somers and his

Brightly-colored parrots at the Aquarium and Zoo will catch the kids' attention.

fellow shipwreck victims. It is almost small enough to be a toy ship.

Aquarium and Zoo. The fish are fascinating (look for the huge moray eel, which is not for the squeamish), but the zoo exhibits are also fun. Talking parrots, peacocks in full display, and cute lemurs will always win hearts.

Crystal Caves. Children will be awestruck by both the size and the beauty of this underground cavern.

Devil's Hole. Feeding sharks and turtles is great fun, and because the hole is round and small, kids can get pretty close to the action. Just make sure that they don't become bait!

Historical re-enactments. In King's Square in St. George's, the demonstrations

This replica of the Deliverance *is a magnet for young explorers.*

of the ducking stools and stocks show that being grounded isn't the worst punishment in the world.

Dolphin Quest (at the Bermuda Maritime Museum, Royal Naval Dockyard). Every child will relish the fun-filled display and the chance to touch these magical creatures.

Helmet diving. A safe option for those too young to dive or snorkel, as well as a wonderful opportunity to experience the underwater environment at close quarters.

EATING OUT

For such a small island, Bermuda has a wealth of dining opportunities—from *haute cuisine* to down-to-earth cafés. International gourmets will have no quarrel with the quality of the new-wave French cooking or the comprehensive wine cellars. There are numerous beautiful restaurants with silver service and attentive waiters, where the elegant décor is matched by your own elegant attire. Most restaurants have a dress code: jackets for men (a few places still expect a tie) and "smart casual" for women. But if you get homesick for hamburgers, pizza, or fish and chips, you have no need to worry. Such familiar fare can be found in bars and cafés across the island.

To support the dining needs of over half-a-million visitors each year along with its own growing population, Bermuda must import a vast percentage of its food. However, there are no corners cut on quality. Only the best ingredients find their way here, which is one reason why budget dining options are very few. Prices range from expensive to moderate.

What to Eat

Unlike its island counterparts in the Caribbean, Bermuda has not developed a range of dishes that could be considered a distinctive cuisine. Nevertheless, there are a number of items that you will find here that will certainly never appear on your menu at home.

Breakfast

Your hotel might offer a Bermuda breakfast. This used to be a compulsory way to start the day but for many islanders is now a Sunday treat. The meal is a nutritionally balanced plate of boiled salt codfish with tomato and onion sauce, boiled potatoes, hard-boiled egg, and a banana on the side.

Soups

Bermuda fish chowder is a highly spiced, thick broth usually served with a dash of sherry pepper sauce and rum. Beyond the principal ingredient—fish heads—the cook employs fresh fish, onions, salt pork, tomatoes, and a garden of herbs. *Conch chowder* is another Bermuda favorite. Aside from the mollusks, it contains celery, onion, tomatoes, potato, salt pork, herbs, and perhaps a dash of cream. *Portuguese red bean soup,* a local standby, sometimes comes as thick and spicy as Texas chili. It's certainly a hearty soup, with kidney beans, potato, tomato, onion, garlic, kale, and chunks of ham and sausage.

Great for people-watching or just watching the sea, Front Street restaurants provide food as good as the views.

A.S. COOPER & SONS LTD.

A nutritious Bermuda breakfast will keep you going no matter how full your plans are for the rest of the day.

Fish and Seafood

Surrounded by miles of ocean with both deep-sea and shallow waters, Bermuda is a fish lover's paradise. In many restaurants the "catch of the day" will be the tastiest and freshest option. Snapper is a very frequent choice but, depending on the season, you might also find tuna, wahoo, or rockfish. Served with a simple butter sauce or more complex wine sauces, the fillets will always be superb. Much of the other fish and seafood on the island is delicious but will often be imported: giant shrimps, scallops, Dover sole, and crab, among others.

The monarch of shellfish in Bermuda waters is the spiny lobster, similar to cold-water lobster except that it lacks biting claws. When the local supply is insufficient, lobster from Maine sometimes appears on menus. The local lobster season runs from September through March. It is served broiled with melted butter, baked in a cheese sauce, or sautéed in chunks with brandy and covered with a cream sauce.

Mussel pie is a favorite Bermuda seafood dish—a slightly curried, thick clam stew in a pastry shell. Another island specialty might sound barbarous but tastes rich: *Bermuda shark.* It reaches the table after several beneficial transformations, arriving in tiny pieces cooked with onions, peppers, parsley, thyme, and mustard greens.

Meat and Vegetables

Meat eaters will find such familiar cuts and dishes as steaks and chops, French-style baby lamb, veal scaloppine, and chicken cacciatore.

The vegetables include some Bermuda specialties. You're likely to encounter a startlingly down-home entry known locally as *peas 'n' rice.* In some Bermuda circles this is called *Hop 'n' John,* and it's so good it can be stretched into a main dish. Aside from the advertised peas and rice, it contains a Bermuda onion, bacon or chicken, and a sliced Portuguese sausage. Those famous onions are featured in many a dish, including *onions in cream* and *onion pie.*

Bermuda Onions

In the 19th century, Bermuda exported the local onions to major markets in the US. Bermuda onions were known for their sweet taste, but the name was never registered as a trademark. Soon other countries were producing "Bermuda onions," and the island's industry collapsed. However, anyone born on the island today is still referred to as an "onion," and you will find the motif all over the island from T-shirt logos to the names of shops and cafés.

Less familiar, perhaps, is the Bermuda *pawpaw,* known elsewhere as papaya and used on the island in a double capacity as both a fruit and a vegetable. Baked *pawpaw* comes out as a creamy, cheesy casserole. Pumpkin, plantain, and *christophene* (a kind of squash) are also dressed up for dinner.

Afternoon Tea

The British custom of having tea, sandwiches, and cakes late in the afternoon has been carried on in Bermuda. But it has been given a twist at many hotels: in the summer months it is served around the pool so that guests don't miss one minute of the wonderful weather.

Desserts

Locally grown fruits are used with abandon in Bermuda. Fruit salads might contain a selection of strawberries, loquats, jumbo grapefruit, watermelon, and Suriname cherries. Bananas are also a popular choice, fried as fritters or flamed in rum for a sumptuous finale to a meal.

In the summer, Bermudians and tourists alike enjoy "snowballs," the tasty crushed and flavored ices sold at stands around the island.

However, the British influence is never seen more clearly in Bermuda than on the dessert menu in restaurants. You will find such traditional "puddings" as jelly-roll or sponge cake drowned in sherry and laden with peaches or strawberries, bananas, chopped nuts, custard, and whipped cream. But you will also encounter the lighter Bermudian *syllabub:* guava jelly, port or sherry, and whipped cream.

Christmas brings out Bermuda's national dish, *cassava pie.* Cassava (also known as manioc) was imported from the West Indies in the earliest days of the colony. Here it is combined with chicken, pork, eggs, and perhaps brandy in a sweetish but meaty layered pie. *Sweet potato pudding* — with cinnamon, cloves, and lemon or orange juice to add counterpoint to the yam's bland sweetness — is a favorite for Guy Fawkes Day (5 November).

What to Drink

Before dinner, Bermudians are apt to indulge in a rum drink or two. The distinctive "Black Seal" blend of rum is unique to Bermuda; it is dark and slightly sweeter than other Caribbean rums. The most popular rum drink is the *rum swizzle,* which typically contains light and/or dark rum, bitters, fruit juices (lime, pineapple, orange), and a sweetener

A quintessential Bermudian aperitif: Gosling's rum mixed into sweet swizzles.

such as honey, sugar syrup, or grenadine. With crushed ice, the whole mixture is agitated by inserting a pronged "swizzle" stick into the pitcher and rubbing it between the palms of the hands.

Another locally popular rum drink is the *dark and stormy,* combining rum with the local ginger ale. It is said that a sailor invented the name when he said that the drink was the color of clouds that you wouldn't want to sail toward.

What better place to try one of those tempting concoctions than at the Swizzle Inn itself?

A small brewery produces a variety of microbrew beers with a range of styles and tastes. Bermuda Brewery Company has a range from a dark stout beer to a German-style Pilsner. It also brews its "Hurricane" brew to coincide with the season. Bottled American and other European beers are readily available, as are all the best-known brands of spirits.

With dinner you'll be able to choose from comprehensive wine lists that usually include a reasonably priced carafe. Or choose a soft drink, fruit punch, or Bermudian ginger ale (much spicier than other brews of the same name). Imported mineral water is universally available, although many Bermudians find the idea of drinking bottled water strange since their own rainwater is so pure.

HANDY TRAVEL TIPS

An A–Z Summary of Practical Information

Bermuda

ACCOMMODATION

Bermuda offers a broad range of accommodation, from resort complexes as lavish as any in the world to simple guesthouses. However, the number of rooms in the top bracket far exceeds the choices in the economy class. The Bermuda Department of Tourism lists every registered place to stay in its comprehensive booklet *(Where to Stay in Bermuda),* with each listing featuring a picture and details about the facilities. Visitors are always urged to book early for Bermuda through authorized travel agents.

Hotels and guesthouses of all classes have reduced rates in winter —from November or December to the end of February or mid-March. But note also that entertainment and facilities might be cut back during this low season.

Hotels usually offer a choice among meal plans. The Modified American Plan (MAP) includes breakfast and dinner in the room rate (plus, in some places, a British-style afternoon tea). The so-called Bermuda Plan (BP) covers room and full breakfast only. Housekeeping cottages and guesthouses might offer Bermuda Plan or a slightly stripped-down Continental Plan (CP: room and light breakfast) or European Plan (EP: room only). However, visitors who choose the non-American plans will find no shortage of restaurants of all varieties on the island. Note that in the winter, many of the larger hotels offer a "dine around" plan that allows those staying on a MAP plan to dine at other hotel dining rooms.

The big hotels and many of the smaller establishments advertise special package holidays for honeymooners, golfers, tennis fans, and other special-interest visitors. These usually include extra activities or facilities at little or no additional cost.

Most of the large hotels have shopping arcades, bars, restaurants, tennis courts, and swimming pools on the premises. Some have their own private beaches; others send their guests to beach clubs. The big hotels either have their own golf courses or offer their guests privileges at nearby clubs. The smaller hotels have limited on-site facilities for shopping and entertainment and are less formal.

In cottage colonies—a Bermudian idea—the individual cottages or bungalows are spread out on spacious grounds, with a central main clubhouse, dining room, and bar for those who want to socialize. All have their own beaches or pools but limited entertainment. Cottage colonies can be very luxurious.

Bermuda also has two exclusive club resorts noted for privacy and luxury. You have to be a member (or be introduced by a member) to get a reservation.

For those who want to economize, Bermuda has housekeeping cottages and efficiency apartments. These usually include roomy surroundings with a pool or beach or both. The kitchenettes help to cut down on restaurant bills.

Guesthouses, the least expensive of all, range from old mansions with spacious accommodation to more modest private houses with smaller rooms and even less formality. Some serve breakfast, and a few offer an advantageous Modified American Plan with home-cooked dinners. You will also find guesthouses that offer housekeeping units or shared kitchen facilities.

AIRPORT

There is only one international airport serving Bermuda. Located on St. David's Island, the Bermuda International Airport developed using the same runways as the military planes at the US base, Kindley Field.

Taxis can be found outside the arrivals terminal for the transfer to your hotel. Prices for the journey to Hamilton will be approximately $25 and to Southampton only a little more.

When you leave at the end of your stay, the departure tax from the airport is $29.

B

BICYCLE and MOPED RENTAL/HIRE

Bicycles. Renting a bicycle is a good way to see Bermuda. The island is compact, and automobile drivers are for the most part considerate and careful. The Railway Trail is open to bicyclists, which means a number of miles can be cycled off the main roads. Bicycles can be rented at the same companies that rent mopeds and motorcycles (see below). One slight word of caution: although Bermuda has few hills, using a cycle to get around will involve some pedaling, so it isn't for the totally unfit!

Mopeds. These one- or two-person machines are simple to operate, (with no gears) and are a fun way to travel around the small island's narrow roads. Since the speed limit is 35 km/h (20 mph) for all vehicles, it is relatively safe. Reputable companies will have a protected place for you to practice until you feel comfortable with the bike.

Mopeds can be rented from a number of companies; the minimum age is 16. Your hotel will be able to make suitable arrangements for you. If not, then Oleander Cycles (Gorham Road, Hamilton; Tel: 295-0919; website: <www.oleandercycles.bm>) is a reputable rental company. A single moped rental is about $150 for the first seven days, $12 per day thereafter. Double moped rental is around $200 for the first seven days, $15 per day thereafter. Add a deposit of $20 plus $15 damage waiver to each rental. Prices tend to be similar for every company, so don't worry about shopping around unless you want to.

Helmets and third-party insurance are compulsory.

BUDGETING for YOUR TRIP

Bermuda is a relatively expensive destination. Since there is no income tax for islanders (who "take home" almost all they earn), government revenue is raised by charging duty on goods coming into the island. This includes almost everything, from foodstuffs to furniture.

Hotels. Most hotels offer rooms with a meal plan, so you should always research exactly what is included in the price (see ACCOMMODATION). Double room in a moderate hotel: $175. Double room in an expensive hotel: $300.

Meals. Three-course lunch (without drinks), per person: $30 in a moderate restaurant, $50 in an expensive restaurant.

Golf. Green fees: between $60 and $150 per round, depending on the course and season.

Diving. Single dive with equipment: $50–$70; "Discover Package": $100 for 3 hours.

Boat rental. $500 for 4 hours; $1000 for 8 hours.

Public bus. *Cash:* 3 zones $2.50, 14 zones $4. *Token:* 3 zones $2.25, 14 zones $3.75. *Tickets* (booklets of 15 rides): 3 zones $15, 14 zones $24. *Passes* (unlimited rides, all zones): 1 day $10, 3 days $21, 7 days $34, 1 month $40.

Ferry boat. The longest trip costs $3.75 one way.

Tour by taxi. $20/hr for up to 4 people; $30/hr for 5–6 people.

Arrival. Taxi from the airport to Hamilton: $25.

Departure. Tax of $29 per person, payable in cash at the airport.

CAMPING

Independent travelers may not camp in Bermuda. Between October and April, camping is allowed for organized groups at designated campsites, usually on outlying islands. Details of campsites and fees can be obtained from the Camping Coordinator, Department of Youth and Sport, Old Fire Station Building, 81 Court Street, Hamilton HM12, Bermuda.

Bermuda

CAR RENTAL/HIRE

It is not possible for tourists to rent cars in Bermuda. Those who want to see the island independently will need to rent a bicycle, motor scooter, or moped.

CLIMATE

Bermuda has a temperate subtropical climate aided by the Gulf Stream, which blows north from the Gulf of Mexico. Although the islands lie on the same latitude as North Carolina, they have a warmer climate. There are two main seasons. Summer lasts roughly from April through October, when temperatures reach 30°C (86°F). Winter is from November through March, when the weather might still be fine and warm but strong storms can lash the island. It might rain at all times of year. The following are average figures, which will of course vary.

	J	F	M	A	M	J	J	A	S	O	N	D
°C	19	18	18	19	21	24	30	30	30	24	21	19
°F	66	65	65	66	69	75	86	86	86	75	69	66

CLOTHING

Clothing. Bermuda still has many conservative social habits, especially where clothing is concerned. "Smart casual" is the term seen in many restaurants, bars, and hotel lobbies to indicate no beach wear and no bare feet. When in town, skimpy clothing is frowned upon.

Bermuda shorts are almost a uniform for the men of the island, but there are strict rules about the length and styling. Shorts should be no more than 7.5 cm (3 inches) above the knee; they are always worn with long socks.

Formal dress is favored at all soirées and for dinner in the most fashionable hotels. At the very least, men must wear a jacket; a tie is sometimes compulsory, but this rule is slowly relaxing. Women must be "smart casual," which means dressing for dinner. When making a reservation at a restaurant, it is always wise to inquire about the dress code.

The Bermudian social set enjoys dressing up, so on Saturday nights and on occasions such as Cup Matches, you find very elegant couples dressed "to the nines." To feel fully part of the crowd, take your best clothing along. You will always find a reason to wear that gown hanging at the back of your closet.

For visitors, summer normally provides few problems. The balmy air invites light clothing: swimwear for the beach, cool cottons for sightseeing, elegant linens or silk for the evening. Winter poses a bigger problem, as temperatures can vary greatly depending on the prevailing winds and fronts. It is always best to prepare for a cool spell with a warm sweater, coat, or raincoat.

Sightseeing and walking, perhaps along the Railway Trail, require stout comfortable shoes, but don't forget to pack a fancier pair for the evening.

COMPLAINTS

Complaints should always be taken up with the person or organization concerned. If you cannot resolve the situation, then explain the problem to the Bermuda Department of Tourism. The main office is at Global House, on Church Street in Hamilton.

CONSULATES and HIGH COMMISSIONS

Because Bermuda is not an independent nation, there are not many consulates or commissions on the island. It is best to contact the local Bermuda-related offices in your home country.

Canada. Canadian Consulate General (Commission to Bermuda), 1251 Avenue of the Americas, New York, NY 10020, US; Tel: (212) 596-1700; fax: (212) 596-1790.

Ireland. Windsor Place, 18 Queen Street, Hamilton HM 11; Tel: 295-6574.

Bermuda

US. American Consulate General, Crown Hill, 16 Middle Road, Devonshire Parish (mailing address: P.O. Box HM 325, Hamilton HM BX, Bermuda); Tel: 295-1342; fax: 295-1592.

CRIME and SAFETY

Bermuda has far less major crime than other destinations, and there are isn't the ominous atmosphere one finds on some Caribbean islands. It is safe to walk or jog alone on beaches and to walk around towns in the evening. However, petty crime is a factor and should always be guarded against. Do not abandon common sense just because you are on vacation. Always leave valuables in the hotel safe, lock your bike when you leave it parked, and do not wander alone at night in unlit places.

CUSTOMS and ENTRY REQUIREMENTS

Visitors from the US and Canada require identification (birth certificate, naturalization certificate, or passport) to enter Bermuda. All other visitors need a valid passport. Visas are required by nationals of some countries so check with your local Bermuda representative.

Visitors may stay in Bermuda for up to 21 days; extensions are granted only by the Department of Immigration. All visitors must complete a declaration form for the customs and immigration authorities, including the address at which they will reside during their stay. Everyone arriving in Bermuda must have a return or onward ticket.

US dollars are accepted all across the island as equivalent to the Bermuda dollar. This is thus a sensible currency to use throughout your stay. There are no currency restrictions in Bermuda. You may change any Bermuda dollars you have back to US dollars before you leave the island.

Visitors entering Bermuda may bring items for personal use along with the following items duty-free: 1.137 liters (1 quart) of wine, 1.137 liters (1 quart) of spirits, 0.454 kg (1 lb) of tobacco, 50 cigars, and up to $30 worth of gifts.

Tourists returning to or traveling on to the United States will be able to clear US customs before they leave Bermuda.

D

DRIVING

Although you won't be able to drive a car in Bermuda, it's still important to know the main driving rules, especially if you intend to rent a motorcycle or bicycle.

Bermudians drive on the left. Road conditions are good even though roads are narrow, undulating, and twisting. The island-wide speed limit is 35 km/h (20 mph), but some local people drive faster. Drivers are generally courteous and patient. Horns only seem to be used to greet passing friends and colleagues. All distance signs are in kilometers and fuel is sold in liters.

Parking restrictions operate in Hamilton and St. George's at peak times. This means that in certain areas only residents or permit holders may park, or that parking is granted only for a restricted length of time. Always watch for small information signs that will inform you of any restrictions for the area where you have parked.

All fuel stations are open 7am–7pm daily, although some will be open later into the evening. Fuel can be found on the main roads linking the towns.

Fluid measures

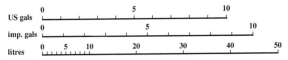

Distance

E

ELECTRICITY

Bermuda operates on a 110-volt/60-cycle AC system, which is the same as the rest of North America. All other visitors will need adapters for their appliances.

EMERGENCIES

To contact the police or fire departments, dial 911. Police head-quarters tel: 295-0011.

G

GAY and LESBIAN TRAVELERS

Because Bermuda is still a rather traditional and conservative place, there is virtually no gay "scene" on the island.

GETTING THERE

By air. There are regularly scheduled flights to Bermuda from the US, Canada, and the UK. It is a relatively short flight for most visitors from the US East Coast, allowing you to arrive fresh enough for an afternoon round of golf. Canadian travelers can reach Bermuda on regular flights from Toronto or via a connection through a US hub.

For British, Irish, and European travelers, British Airways operates a regular service connecting with flights from all major European destinations. Flights depart from London Gatwick Airport. Flying from a European city to the US and then on to Bermuda can sometimes offer a more flexible option, with more carriers from which to choose.

The major airlines serving Bermuda:

Air Canada: Tel: 293-0793, 800-776-3000 (toll-free in US).

American: Tel: 293-1420, 800-433-7300 (toll-free in US).

British Airways: Tel: 295-4422, 800-247-9297 (toll-free in US), 0845 77 333 77 (in UK).

Continental: Tel: 800-231-0856 (toll-free in US), 0800-776-464 (toll-free in UK).

Delta: Tel: 293-1022, 800-221-1212 (toll-free in US), 0800-414-767 (toll-free in UK).

US Airways: Tel: 293-3072, 800-622-1015 (toll-free in US).

By sea. For many decades Bermuda has been a premier cruise destination. Ships departing from New York operate from April to October. A seven-day cruise from New York will typically allow 36 hours in Bermuda. Shorter or longer itineraries are available depending on the cruise line and the length of trip you want to take. Cruise ships dock at different ports (Bermuda Dockyard, Hamilton, and St. George's); if you have a preference, check on the itinerary before making a firm booking.

The following cruise lines have regular service to Bermuda:

Celebrity Cruises: Tel: 800-437-3111 (toll-free in US), 0500-332-232 (toll-free in UK); website <www.celebrity-cruises.com>.

Norwegian Cruise Line: Tel: 800-327-7030 (toll-free in US), 0800-181-560 (toll-free in UK); website <www.ncl.com>.

Royal Caribbean Cruise Line: Tel: 800-327-6700 (toll-free in US), 0500-212-213 (toll-free in UK); website <www.rccl.com>.

GUIDES and TOURS

Bermuda taxi drivers (over 600 of them) are said to be the friendliest and best informed of any in the world. But to be sure, book a taxi with a blue flag. These individuals are qualified guides and can be booked by the hour for tours; the current rate is $20/hr. Taxis can be booked through your hotel's reception desk.

There is one wheelchair-accessible taxi, operated by Sam Matthews (Tel: 234-7205); other large taxis can take disabled travelers with wheelchairs stored in the back.

Bermuda

For customized guided walking tours, contact Bermuda Lectures and Tours (Tel: 234-4082; fax: 238-2773).

H

HEALTH and MEDICAL CARE

Bermuda has few health worries. Its lack of ragweed means that it is often a place of refuge for hay fever sufferers. What problems there are can be avoided by taking appropriate cautions.

Precautions. Especially in the winter months, jellyfish float on the water or are washed up on beaches. Several species have stings that can be harmful. When diving or snorkeling, avoid stepping on the spines of sea urchins; these can become embedded in the flesh.

To avoid sunburn and even sunstroke, avoid too much sun on the first few days of your trip. You should also avoid too much alcohol, which can lead to dehydration when combined with heat and sunshine.

Every year a number of visitors fall from mopeds and bicycles, suffering what is known by the locals as "road rash": large scrapes caused by skin hitting the road surface. To minimize your risk, wear a covering of clothing when traveling (ideally slacks and a long sleeved shirt). Crash helmets are required by law and help to guard against head injury.

Medical care. If you do have a health problem, most hotels will have a doctor on call, and all should be able to make arrangements for a doctor to visit you. All doctors and dentists on Bermuda operate private practices, so you will need to pay for consultation and treatment.

Bermuda has one hospital, King Edward VII Memorial Hospital (Tel: 236-2345), with 55 doctors and a number of specialists. The 24-hour emergency department can deal with unforeseen health problems. All visitors are required to pay in advance for medical care, and it is imperative that you have adequate insurance to cover any treatment that you might need. For minor medical problems, you will need to pay for your treatment and then be reimbursed by your insurance company when you return home.

Those who take prescription medicines should always carry enough to meet their needs. Overseas prescriptions will not be honored in Bermuda. Pharmacies are stocked with many internationally recognized brand names for minor ailments, but prices will be higher than at home.

The water is safe to drink, as is the ice in drinks.

HOLIDAYS

(Public holidays that fall on a Sunday are normally observed the following day, which means offices will remain closed on Monday.)

New Year's Day	1 January
Good Friday	(variable) generally in April
Bermuda Day	24 May
Queen's Official Birthday	third Monday in June
Cup Match Day	(variable) late July/early August
Somers Day	day after Cup Match Day
Labour Day	first Monday in September
Remembrance Day	11 November
Christmas Day	25 December
Boxing Day	26 December

L

LANGUAGE

English is the official language of Bermuda, spoken with a unique accent and with British spellings and vocabulary. You will also hear some special words from Caribbean English.

LAUNDRY and DRY CLEANING

Most large hotels offer laundry and dry cleaning services. However, there are several reliable dry cleaners and laundries on the island if you want to deposit your own items for cleaning:

Blue Ribbon Dry Cleaners, 8 Bermudiana Road, Hamilton; Tel: 296-4265.

Bermuda

Paget Dry Cleaners, at the corner of Lovers' Lane and Middle Road, Paget Parish; Tel: 235-5142.

Touch of Class, 60 Water Lane East, St. George's; Tel: 297-8238.

MAPS

The Bermuda Department of Tourism produces a basic map of the islands, with detailed plans of Hamilton, St. George's, and the Royal Naval Dockyard along with the main attractions and golf courses. But this map does not include bus routes. A separate bus and ferry timetable (with map) can be obtained from the visitor's information offices, hotels, and in Hamilton at the ferry terminal on Front Street and at the bus terminal next to the City Hall.

On the Internet, you can view various Bermuda maps at the following websites: <www.bermuda.com>, <www.bermuda.bm>, <www.insiders.com/bermuda>.

MEDIA

The only daily newspaper on Bermuda is the *Royal Gazette.* There are also two weeklies: the *Bermuda Sun* and the *Mid Ocean News.* The bi-weekly Bermuda Times concentrates on community events. Most of the major US daily newspapers will be available in hotel lobbies or gift shops; they usually arrive on the day of publication. Major British newspapers are more difficult to find.

Bermuda Broadcasting operates the ZBM and ZFB radio and TV stations. Most hotels carry the major US TV networks along with various cable channels. The BBC World News service is also available at certain hotels. On Bermuda's televisions, Channel 11 carries continuous weather forecasts.

MONEY MATTERS

Currency. Bermuda's currency is the Bermuda dollar, which is officially linked to the US dollar in terms of daily fluctuations. American currency is interchangeable with Bermuda currency on the island, although vendors are not obliged to take it. You might receive your change in a mixture of local and US bills and coins. (Be sure to convert all your Bermuda money before you leave the island.)

Banknotes: $2, $5, $20, $50, $100. Coins:1¢, 5¢, 10¢, 25¢, and $1. Coins are the same size as their American equivalents, with the profile of Queen Elizabeth II on the front and island designs on the reverse side.

Banks. Bermuda's three banks (and their branch offices) are open from 9:30am to 3pm Mon–Fri, with an extra hour for late business from 4:30pm to 5:30pm every Friday. Although this is a small, isolated island, the banks are superbly qualified to carry out all types of sophisticated international transactions.

There is also a network of international automatic teller machines (ATMs) that will take Honor and Cirrus cards along with major credit cards.

Traveler's checks. In US-dollar denominations, traveler's checks are accepted everywhere. The banks can cash checks in all other currencies.

Credit cards. The major international credit cards are accepted in many shops as well as in restaurants and hotels.

 O

OPENING HOURS

Offices are open Mon–Fri 9am–5pm. Shops are generally open 9am–5pm. In addition, shopping hours are extended during the summer (Apr–Oct), especially on Harbour Nights in Hamilton and Heritage Nights in St. George's. Major grocery stores are open until 10pm.

Bermudians still observe Sunday as a day of rest, so most shops and all offices are closed that day. During the week, some shops and post offices will close for lunch, especially in the smaller villages, but this practice is slowly changing.

P

POLICE

Bermuda's unarmed police officers, in their constable helmets and Bermuda shorts, are a tourist attraction in themselves. They are recruited in Britain and the West Indies as well as locally. You should address a policeman or policewoman as "Officer." They're quite cordial about answering questions, giving directions, and even posing for pictures.

POST OFFICES

Post offices are found in every parish. They are open from 8am to 5pm Mon–Fri (the smaller ones close for lunch). The General Post Office at Church and Parliament streets in Hamilton is also open on Saturdays, from 8am until noon.

On the streets, mail may be dropped into the British-style red pillar boxes with monograms of Queen Elizabeth II or earlier monarchs.

Postage. Although letters and postcards sent at surface rates normally go to and from Bermuda by air, those marked "Airmail" and with the correct postage will take priority.

Rates for postcards: 70¢ to the US and Canada, 80¢ to other destinations (including Britain and Europe). Postcards can take up to seven days to reach North American destinations and a little longer to Europe.

PUBLIC TRANSPORTATION

Bus system. Bermuda has a comprehensive public transport system that is clean and safe; it also runs on time. Most services operate from 7am–11pm, with more limited hours on Sundays. On an island where only one car is allowed for each household, buses are used regularly by the local population.

The bus network covers the island and takes you directly (or very close) to most of the major attractions. All bus routes begin at the terminal in Hamilton between Church and Victoria streets, next to City Hall.

Routes are numbered from 1 to 11, with the final destination indicated in a box above the front windshield. You can stop any bus at bus stops marked by blue and pink poles situated at the side of the road. Poles with pink tops indicate a route in to Hamilton; poles with a blue top indicate a route out of Hamilton.

Bus routes are split into a number of zones, and the price of the journey reflects the number of zones you traverse. Any trip over three zones is considered a 14-zone journey. There are several methods of payment. Cash can be used, but it must be in coins (not bills) and must be exact, as drivers do not return change. This makes cash the least practical method of payment (it is also the most expensive option).

If you pay in cash, a 3-zone fare is $2.50, and a 14-zone fare is $3.75. A cheaper method is to purchase tickets in advance in books of fifteen tickets: $15 for fifteen 3-zone tickets and $24 for fifteen 14-zone tickets. Tokens in the shape of metal coins can be bought for 2-, 3-, or 14-zone trips: $2.25 for 3 zones, $3.75 for 14 zones.

The most economical discount is the pass. Passes for 1 day ($10), 3 days ($21), 7 days ($34), 1 month ($40), or 3 months offer unlimited travel on buses. Both passes and tokens may also be used on the ferries. Many large hotels will sell 1-, 3-, and 7-day passes along with tokens and tickets. Passes for lengthier periods are available at the central bus terminal.

Ferries. For over 200 years, Bermuda has had ferry boats. Today there is a limited but regular service from Hamilton Harbour to ports on the south side of the island. Ferry stops are at small harbors along the Paget and Warwick coastlines (across the bay from Hamilton) as well as at Somerset and Dockyard. During the summer, a ferry service also links Dockyard with St. George's for a whole day of water transport and historical sightseeing from Bermuda's western to eastern tips. Ferries can also take bicycles or motor bikes for a combination of road and water travel. The one-way fare from Hamilton to Dockyard (via Somerset) is $3.75; mopeds are $3.75 each, and bicycles are carried free.

Bermuda

A comprehensive route guide for both buses and ferries can be obtained from the tourist information offices and from hotels and bus terminals (see also <www. bermudabuses.com>).

Minibuses. A minibus service operates in the East End of the island, serving the outskirts of St. George's and St. David's. It is available 7am–11pm every 15 minutes, departing from King's Square. Fares for travel around St. George's is $1.75 per journey. One-hour tours of the town of St. George's are also available from King's Square.

A minibus service operates in the West End from Somerset Bridge to the Royal Naval Dockyard, serving all of Somerset, Boaz , and Ireland islands. The bus operates daily 8:30am–5:30pm, although service is sometimes decreased between December and March. Ticket prices range from $2 to $3 per person per journey.

Carriages. During the summer, horse-drawn carriages may be hired for tours of Hamilton or romantic rides around the island. These can be booked through your hotel or on Front Street, where the carriages depart. The price for up to four passengers is around $20 for 30 minutes.

R

RELIGION

Bermuda's residents are predominantly Christian, with Anglicanism the largest denomination. But there are nearly 20 denominations represented and over 140 churches where worship takes place regularly. Sunday is still spent as a day of rest by the majority of Bermudians.

T

TELEPHONE

The access code from outside Bermuda is 441. All local telephone numbers for the island have seven digits.

If you wish to make an overseas phone call from Bermuda, first dial 00 and then add the country code before dialing the number (with the appropriate area code where necessary).

Most hotels will have in-room telephones for direct-dial calls. Note that these calls will be charged at premium rates. It is far cheaper to use the phone booths that can be found all over the island as well as in hotel lobbies. These take prepaid cards in the amounts of $10, $20, and $50 for direct calls; the rates are far cheaper than calls from hotels. Cards can be bought in stores all across Bermuda.

There are also a small number of telephones that will link directly to AT&T, MCI, and Sprint. These are located at the ferry/cruise docks at Hamilton, Dockyard, and St. George's.

For the hearing impaired, Bermuda operates an IDD system to over 150 countries.

International Access Codes: AT&T: 1-800 872-2881; MCI: 1-800 888-8000 (C&W); or 1-800 888 8888 (TBI); Sprint: 1-800 623 0877.

TIME ZONES

Bermuda operates on Atlantic Time, which is four hours behind Greenwich Mean Time (GMT-4) and one hour ahead of US Eastern Standard Time. The following chart shows the times in various cities in the winter:

San Francisco	New York	*Bermuda*	London	Sydney
8am	11am	*noon*	4pm	1am

TIPPING

In most bars and restaurants, a gratuity will automatically be added to your bill. Many hotels will add a service charge to your room rate.When you arrive at your hotel, ask about the policy for maid and bar service. Taxi drivers should be tipped 10 percent of the fare.

TOILETS

There are free, clean public toilets at a number of places around Bermuda. At the three major tourist destinations, you will find toilets

Bermuda

at King's Square in St. George's, the Clocktower Shopping Mall at the Royal Naval Dockyard, and in Hamilton at Par-la-Ville Park and at the Ferry Dock.

TOURIST INFORMATION OFFICES

The Bermuda Department of Tourism operates offices in Bermuda as well as around the world.

Head Office
Global House, 43 Church Street, Hamilton; Tel: 292-0023.

Bureaus around Bermuda
Ferry Terminal Building, 8 Front Street, Hamilton; Tel: 295-1480. Open Mon–Sat 9am–2pm.

7 King's Square, St. George's; Tel: 297-1642. Open Mon–Sat 9:30am–2pm.

Royal Naval Dockyard; Tel: 234-3824. Open Mon–Fri 9:30am–3pm, Sun 12pm–4pm.

In the US
New York: 205 East 42nd Street, New York, NY 10017; Tel: (212) 818-9800, 800-223-6106 (toll-free in US).

Boston: 184 High Street, 4th Floor, Boston, MA 02110; Tel: (617) 422-5892.

Los Angeles: 269 South Beverly Drive, PMB 448, Beverly Hills, CA 90212; Tel: 800 223-6106.

Atlanta: 245 Peachtree Center Avenue NE, Suite 803, Atlanta, GA 30303; Tel: (404) 524-1541.

In Canada
1200 Bay Street, Suite 1004, Toronto, Ontario M5R 2A5; Tel: (416) 923-9600.

Serving the UK and Europe
1 Battersea Church Road, London SW11 3LY; Tel: (020) 7771-7001.

The Department of Tourism produces a number of brochures with information about golfing breaks, weddings, and honeymooning as well as general information about hotels, restaurants, and what to do. The website is <**www.bermudatourism.com**>.

Other websites that will help you plan your trip include:
<**www.bermuda.com**>
<**www.bermuda-online.org**>
<**www.inbermuda.com**>
<**www.insiders.com/bermuda**>

WEIGHTS and MEASURES

Bermuda is slowly converting from imperial measure (feet, miles, pounds, and gallons) to the metric system, so you will find both systems in use.

Length

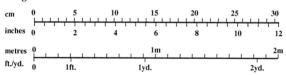

Weight

Temperature

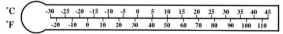

Recommended Hotels

Bermuda offers a wide choice of accommodation in terms of both style and price, from luxurious resorts with comprehensive facilities to more modest hotels and guesthouses, some with a "colonial" feel. There is very little choice in the budget sector of the market, with prices higher than at mainland US hotels.

Many hotels welcome children and have special programs for them, but others have a policy of not catering to young children.

There are several meal options when booking a room. See ACCOMMODATION, page 110.

The following selection of hotels covers a range of accommodation options. Prices quoted are in US dollars per room (double occupancy). Unless otherwise indicated, all rooms provide air-conditioning and TV. Many hotels will add a service charge of 15 percent and an occupancy tax of 7.25 percent. Prices can vary enormously between high and low season, with summer generally being the most expensive.

$$$$	above $200
$$$	$150–$200
$$	$100–$150
$	under $100

Ariel Sands $$$$ *P.O. Box 334, Hamilton HM BX; Tel: 236-1010, 800-468-6610 (toll-free in US); fax: 236-0087; website <www.arielsands.com>.* A cottage colony set in manicured lawns with a natural ocean-fed pool and pristine beach. Spa treatments and exercise room, tennis courts, Caliban's beachside restaurant with outdoor dining and Calypso music. 51 rooms. Major credit cards.

Cambridge Beaches $$$$ *King's Point Road, Somerset MA 02; Tel: 234-0331, 800-468-7300 (toll-free in US), 800-463-5990 (toll-free in Canada); fax: 234-3352; website <www.cambridge-beaches.com>.* This cottage colony has recently completed an extensive renovation program. Set on a peninsula with five private beaches overlooking Mangrove and Long Bay in Sandys Parish. "Aquarian Baths" featuring indoor and exercise pools, gym, solarium, and hot tub. Complimentary ferry service to Hamilton. Windsurfing, snorkeling, and fishing available. Guests are automatically members of all Bermuda golf courses. Rooms and suites are cottage style with full range of amenities offering privacy and luxury. 81 rooms. Major credit cards.

Clear View Suites $$ *Sandy Lane, Hamilton Parish CR 02; Tel: 293-0484, 800-468-9600 (toll-free in US); fax: 293-0267.* Waterfront property set above the Railway Trail in secluded grounds, on main bus route from Hamilton to St. George's. Two heated swimming pools, one tennis court. Each room has a kitchenette plus terrace or patio. 12 rooms. Major credit cards.

Elbow Beach Bermuda $$$$ *P.O. Box HM 455, Hamilton HM BX. Tel: 236-3535, 800-344-3526 (toll-free in US); fax: 236-8043; website <www.elbowbeach.com>.* Situated on a prime South Shore location with one of the best pink beaches on the island and a vast, lush botanical garden. Large, heated freshwater pool with shallow play area for children; beauty salon; health club with Jacuzzi, massage and facials; shopping arcade with a selection of fine stores. Five championship tennis courts; nearby golf courses. Nightly entertainment and dancing. 250 rooms. Major credit cards.

Fairmont Hamilton Princess $$$$ *P.O. Box HM 837, Hamilton HM CX; Tel: 800-441-1414 (toll-free in US and Canada), (44) 20 7389 1126 (in UK and Europe); fax: 506-877-3160; website <www.fairmont.com>.* A large resort hotel at the edge of Hamilton Harbour and within walking distance of central Hamilton, offering classical European elegance with Bermudian atmosphere. Heated pool with patio on harbor's edge, shopping arcade, beauty salon, and complimentary use of fitness center. Ferry transportation to private Fairmont Southampton Princess Beach Club. Restaurants include the renowned Harley's Bistro. 413 rooms. Major credit cards.

Fairmont Southampton Princess $$$$ *P.O. Box HM 1379, Hamilton HM FX; Tel: 800-441-1414 (toll-free in US and Canada); (44) 20 7389 1126 (in UK and Europe); fax: 506-877-3160; website <www.fairmont.com>.* Perched atop the highest point in Bermuda, with panoramic views across the island. Secluded private beach, indoor pool with whirlpool jets, outdoor pool and sundeck, fitness center, spa, beauty salon, 11 all-weather tennis courts, and shopping mall. An 18-hole par-3 executive golf course surrounds the hotel. All rooms have private balcony. Restaurants include casual brasseries, gourmet restaurants, and grill bars. 593 rooms. Major credit cards.

Fourways Inn $$$ *P.O. Box PG 294, Paget PG BX; Tel: 236-6517, 800-962-7654 (toll-free in US); fax: 236-5528; e-mail <fourways@ibl.bm>.* Luxury cottages set in landscaped grounds, near ferry and bus stops. Heated swimming pool, luxury restaurant with pianist nightly. All rooms with private patio. 10 rooms. Major credit cards.

Mid Ocean Club $$$$ *P.O. Box HM 1728, Hamilton HM GX; Tel: 293-0330; fax: 293-8837; e-mail <midoceanclub @ibl.bm>.* A large, exclusive estate on the ocean's edge in Tucker's Town, with three large beaches and numerous private coves. Private, members-only 18-hole championship golf course and tennis courts. 20 rooms. Major credit cards.

Newstead Hotel $$$ *P.O. Box PG 196, Paget PG BX; Tel: 236-6060, 800-468-4111 (toll-free in US); fax: 236-7454; e-mail <reservations@newsteadhotel.com>.* Situated on Harbour Road overlooking Hamilton Harbour near the ferry stop, this Bermuda manor house is in a quiet residential area surrounded by well-groomed houses. Heated pool, sun patio, sauna bath, sailboat rentals from private dock, two tennis courts, and putting green. Weekly barbecue dinners in the summer and Jazz brunch on Sundays. 43 rooms. Major credit cards accepted.

Oxford House $$ *P.O. Box HM 374, Hamilton HM BX; Tel: 295-0503, 800-548-7758 (toll-free in US), 800-272-2306 (toll-free in Canada); fax: 295-0250.* A charming award-winning bed-and-breakfast within a two-minute walk of downtown Hamilton. Large, light-filled accommodation includes doubles, triples, and quads. Homely atmosphere and plenty of personal attention. 12 rooms. Major credit cards.

Pompano Beach Club $$$ *36 Pompano Beach Road, Southampton SB 03; Tel: 234-0222, 800-343-4155 (toll-free in US and Canada); fax: 234-1694; website <www.pompano.bm>.* Overlooking the ocean on the southwest coast with dramatic views from all rooms. Small private beach with excellent snorkeling and watersports facilities, oceanside freshwater heated swimming pool and two Jacuzzis, Port Royal Golf Course (next door), Cedar Room Restaurant overlooking the sea, and complimentary shuttle bus to main road to connect with scheduled bus services. All rooms with sitting area and terrace. 56 rooms. Major credit cards.

The Reefs $$$$ *56 South Road, Southampton SN 02; Tel: 238-0222, 800-742-2008 (toll-free in US and Canada); fax: 238-8372; website <www.thereefs.com>.* Situated on a cliffside overlooking Christian Bay with its own private beach. Rooms and cottages are on several levels between beach and clubhouse; all have ocean views. Freshwater pool and sun patio, two all-weather tennis courts, fitness center, Coconuts Beach restaurant (open summer only), renowned open-air dining, complimentary afternoon tea, gift shop. 65 rooms. Major credit cards.

Rosedon $$ *P.O. Box HM 290, Hamilton HM AX; Tel: 295-1640, 800-742-5008 (toll-free in US); fax: 295-5904; website <www.rosedonbermuda.com>.* Located on the outskirts of Hamilton, this colonial-style house has a wide veranda over-looking gardens. Two large lounges with self-service bar, heated freshwater pool, sun terrace, and local entertainment once per week. 43 rooms. Major credit cards.

Rosemont $ *P.O. HM 37, Hamilton HM AX; Tel: 292-1055, 800-367-0040 (toll-free in US); fax: 295-3913; e-mail <rosemont@ibl.bm>.* Family-run property set on hillside with beautiful landscaped gardens and views over Hamilton Harbour. A five-minute walk from the center of Hamilton. Large pool and sundeck. All rooms with kitchenette and patio. 47 cottages. Major credit cards.

Royal Palms Hotel $$ *P.O. HM 499, Hamilton HM CX; Tel: 292-1854, 800-678-0783 (toll-free in US), 800-799-0824 (toll-free in Canada); fax: 292-1946; <www.royalpalms.bm>.* A short walk from the center of Hamilton, this gracious estate has been restored and turned into an award-winning and intimate hotel that is family-owned and operated, with Bermudian architecture in a tranquil setting. Freshwater pool; Ascot's Restaurant and Bar looks out over the grounds. 25 rooms. Major credit cards.

Sonesta Beach Resort $$$$ *P.O. Box HM 1070, Hamilton HM EX; Tel: 238-8122, 800-SONESTA (toll-free in US); fax: 238-8463; website <www.sonesta.com>.* A modern, luxury resort hotel with a dramatic setting on the South Shore in

Southampton Parish, including 25 acres of landscaped grounds surrounding three natural bays with private beaches. Unique solar dome pool, renowned European health spa and salon, three restaurants, afternoon tea, dancing in the Boat Bay Club, six floodlit tennis courts, scuba facilities with instructors, and "Just Us Kids" summer program. 403 rooms. Major credit cards.

Stonington Beach Hotel $$$ *P.O. Box HM 523, Hamilton HM CX; Tel: 236-5416, 800-457-400 (nationwide and Canada); website <www.stoningtonbeach.com>.* Overlooking the South Shore and a secluded beach in Paget Parish, this is a low-rise hotel set in manicured gardens. Freshwater pool, two all-weather tennis courts, nearby golf course, sundeck dining in the Norwood Room, weekly "rum swizzle" receptions with piano and jazz. 67 rooms. Major credit cards.

Surf Side Beach Club $$ *P.O. Box WK 101, Warwick, WK BX; Tel: 236-7100; 800-553-9990 (toll-free in US); fax: 236-9765; website <www.surfside.bm>.* Terraced landscaped grounds with cottages and apartments overlooking the ocean, with steps down to private beach. A three-minute walk to bus services to Hamilton or Dockyard. Large sun terrace, pool, small fitness center, poolside restaurant. All rooms with kitchen and private veranda. 35 rooms. Major credit cards.

White Sands Hotel and Cottages $$$ *P.O. Box PG 174, Paget PG BX; Tel: 236-2023; 800-548-0547 (toll-free in US); 800-228-3196 (toll-free in Canada); fax: 236-2486; website <www.white-sands-bermuda.com>.* Set on the South Shore, this small intimate hotel stands in groomed grounds and has a relaxed atmosphere. Large lounge and outdoor terrace overlooking the ocean, dining room, and pub-type bar. All rooms with terrace. 35 rooms. Major credit cards.

Recommended Restaurants

In Bermuda, you'll discover a good choice of restaurants offering both local and international cuisine. Most of the larger
resort hotels have acclaimed dining rooms, but there are
also many independent establishments with top reputations
and a faithful clientele.

It is always advisable to make a reservation at restaurants
in Bermuda, especially in the summer and on weekends.
Bermudians enjoy dining out, and you might find it more difficult than you think to get a table at the best establishments.
Be sure to inquire about the dress code at the establishment
where you make a booking (see page 114).

The following price categories are based on a three-
course dinner, per person, without drinks; prices are in US
dollars. Most restaurants will automatically add a 15 percent
gratuity to the bill.

$$$$	$75–$100
$$$	$45–$75
$$	$30–$45
$	below $30

The Bombay $$ *75 Reid Street East, 3rd Floor, Hamilton;
Tel: 292-0048.* Over 30 authentic Indian dishes on the menu,
cooked as hot or as mild as you desire. Vegetarian dishes also
available. Lunch served Monday–Friday noon–2:30pm; dinner
served Monday–Saturday 6:30pm–11pm. Major credit cards.

Carriage House $$$ *22 Water Street, St. George's; Tel: 297-
1270/1730.* Located in the center of St. George's (next to the
Carriage Museum) in an 18th-century vaulted brick building
that used to be the Royal Engineer's Warehouse. For alfresco
dining, it has a wharf-side deck where yachts moor. Choose
from Continental specialties including Barbary Duck and prime

rib or such Bermudian favorites as fish chowder. Casual dining surrounded by history. Open daily for lunch 11:30am–4:30pm and dinner 6pm–9:30pm. Major credit cards.

La Coquille $$–$$$ *at the Bermuda Underwater Institute, East Broadway, Pembroke Parish; Tel: 292-6122.* A dining spot with a marine theme and French Provençal cuisine, situated on the waterfront overlooking Hamilton Harbour (you can arrive by boat!); air-conditioned or alfresco dining. Cocktails served at two bars. Open daily for lunch noon–2:45pm and dinner 6:30pm–10:30pm. Major credit cards.

Dennis' Hideaway $$ *Cashew City Road, St. David's Island; Tel: 297-0444.* Be sure to note the phone number, as you should call to make sure the Hideaway is open on the night you wish to dine. Dennis Lamb is a true island character, whose casual eatery turns out his delicious shark hash, conch stew, fish chowder and other seafood dishes. No credit cards.

Flanagan's $$ *Emporium Building, 69 Front Street, Hamilton; Tel: 295-8299.* Bermuda's only authentic Irish pub, with a good selection of hearty, filling meals. State-of-the-art sports bar inside plus terrace balcony overlooking the harbor on Front Street. Friendly, relaxed atmosphere. Live entertainment nightly. Open daily 11am–10:30pm. Major credit cards.

Fourways Inn $$$$ *1 Middle Road, Paget Parish; Tel: 236-6517.* Named for the four original entrances to this property built in 1727, the restaurant has old English charm and architecture. Superb French cuisine and Bermudian dishes, with classical background music as well as a pianist. Jacket requested; reservations advised. Open daily for lunch noon–3pm and dinner 6:30pm–9:45pm. Major credit cards.

The Frog and Onion $$ *Cooperage Building, Royal Naval Dockyard; Tel: 234-2900.* A genuine British pub and restaurant in an 18th-century building once used by the Royal Navy. Flags and standards drape the walls; stone flags and fireplaces complete the setting. A popular place for lunch, offering favorites such as fish and chips and bangers and mash. Live entertainment on Fridays and Saturdays. Open daily 11:30am–9pm. Major credit cards.

Harbourfront $$$ *21 Front Street West, Hamilton; Tel 295-4207.* This restaurant and sushi bar opposite the ferry terminal has an exciting selection of Mediterranean and Japanese dishes. Overlooking Hamilton Harbour, it offers a perfect setting for a comfortable lunch or elegant dinner inside or out on the enclosed terrace. Jacket required for men at dinner. Open for lunch Monday–Saturday 11:30am–5:30pm; dinner 6pm–10pm. Major credit cards.

Henry VIII Pub and Restaurant $$$ *South Shore Road (below Gibb's Hill Lighthouse), Southampton; Tel: 238-1977.* Set in an opulent faux-Tudor manor with décor that Henry himself would feel at home in, this bustling but friendly restaurant serves hearty English feasts with a good selection of meat, fowl, and seafood. Open daily for lunch noon–2:30pm and dinner 6pm–10pm. Major credit cards.

The Hog Penny $$–$$$ *off Front Street on Burnaby Hill, Hamilton; Tel: 292-2534.* A pub/restaurant with a relaxed atmosphere and a wide selection of popular American and English dishes. Nightly live entertainment. Casual dress. Open daily for lunch 11:30am–4pm and dinner 5:30pm–11pm. Major credit cards.

Landfall Restaurant $$–$$$ *at Clear View, North Shore Road, Hamilton Parish; Tel: 293-1322.* Situated in a 200-year-old building and lovingly operated by "Mama," who makes sure that you are served the finest fresh Bermudian fare. Her fish chowder is a must. Charming and very popular with locals. Reservations suggested. Open daily for breakfast, lunch, and dinner 7:30am–9pm. Major credit cards.

Little Venice $$$ *32 Bermudiana Road, Hamilton; Tel: 295-3503.* Very popular Italian restaurant with an extensive pasta menu along with classic and contemporary dishes. A comprehensive list of Italian and collector's wines is available. Free admission to upstairs club for dancing. Open daily for lunch 11am–2:15pm and dinner 6pm–10pm. Major credit cards.

Lobster Pot $$$–$$$$ *6 Bermudiana Road, Hamilton; Tel: 292-6898; fax: 292-6191.* Considered Bermuda's best seafood restaurant, this informal spot with marine décor is equally popular with islanders and visitors. Varied menu with local and imported seafood. Open daily for lunch 11:30am–3pm and dinner 5:30pm–9:30pm. Major credit cards.

M.R. Onions $$ *11 Par-la-Ville Road, Hamilton; Tel: 292-5012; website <www.mronions.com>.* An upbeat restaurant with a menu and prices to suit everyone. Lobster, ribs, and vegetarian choices; finger foods and bar snacks are available. The friendly bar (open till 1am) has Internet and e-mail facilities; entertainment nightly. Open for lunch Monday–Friday only, from noon–5pm; dinner served nightly 5pm–10pm. Major credit cards.

Ms. Softy's $ *235 Middle Road, Southampton; Tel: 238-0931.* A typical Bermudian meeting place specializing in home-made, hearty dishes. Reasonable prices and interesting conversation: you'll be able to hear all the island gossip. Cod fish and potatoes are a Sunday specialty. Open for breakfast and lunch Monday–Saturday 6am–3pm and Sunday 6am–noon. Cash only.

Tom Moore's Tavern $$$$ *on Walsingham Bay, Hamilton Parish; Tel: 293-8020; website <www.tommoores.com>.* Bermuda's oldest eating establishment was built in 1652 and still has many original features, including windows and fireplaces. You can dine in splendid surroundings on classical French cuisine. It is claimed that two million people have dined here. Jacket and reservations required. Open daily for dinner 7pm–9pm. Major credit cards.

Newport Room $$$–$$$$ *at the Fairmont Southampton Princess Hotel, Southampton Parish; Tel: 238-2555.* Intimate and elegant dining, featuring a creative contemporary French menu and fine vintage wines. The unique ambiance re-creates the interior of a luxury sailing yacht, with crystal and linen tableware. Jacket and tie required; reservations suggested. Open daily (Jun–Sept) for dinner 6:30pm–9:30pm. Major credit cards.

Paw Paws $$ *87 South Road, Warwick; Tel: 236-7459.* French and Bermudian combinations using local ingredients. Favorites include mussel pie and fish cakes (a Sunday specialty). The bar is a popular local meeting place. Open daily for lunch 11am–5pm and dinner 5pm–10pm. Major credit cards.

Pickled Onion $$ *53 Front Street, Hamilton; Tel: 295-2263.* A mix of American and Bermudian dishes, including wahoo and fish chowder, Angus steaks, and baby back ribs. Eat either outside on the balcony overlooking Hamilton Harbour or inside in the lounge bar, where live music is performed nightly after 9pm. A smart, casual place to enjoy a meal and music. Open daily 11:30am–1am. Major credit cards.

Rosa's Cantina $$ *121 Front Street, Hamilton; Tel: 295-1912.* This is big-time Tex-Mex country, with good-sized portions and reasonable prices. Menu includes Texas-style steaks and chicken and Mexican specialties spiced to your taste. A comfortable and friendly restaurant with a relaxed dress code. Take-out service available. Open daily noon–1am. Major credit cards.

Seahorse Grill $$$–$$$$ *at the Elbow Beach Resort, South Shore Road, Paget Parish; Tel: 236-3535.* Contemporary grill that uses fresh local ingredients to fuse modern techniques and Bermudian flavors. Views over the southern coastline from the covered and open terraces. Reservations suggested. Open daily for lunch 11am–3pm and dinner 6pm–10pm. Major credit cards.

The Swizzle Inn $$ *Blue Hole Hill, Bailey's Bay, Hamilton Parish; Tel: 293-9300; website <www.swizzleinn.com>.* Bermuda's oldest pub and the home of the "swizzle" cocktail. An informal landmark located near Crystal Caves en route to the airport. Serves good local and pub fare including fish and chips, conch, steaks, and curry. Dine inside or on the patio or terrace. Open daily 11am–1am (times might vary in winter). Major credit cards.

Tio Pepe $$–$$$ *117 South Shore Road, Southampton Parish (opposite Horseshoe Bay); Tel: 238-1897.* Traditional Italian cooking in a restaurant with a Spanish flair. Seasonal favorites (Sept–Mar) are lobster and Spanish-style suckling pig. Dine inside or on the two outdoor terraces. Open daily for lunch noon–5pm and dinner 5pm–10pm. Major credit cards.

La Trattoria $$$ *22 Washington Lane, Hamilton; Tel: 295-1877.* Red-checked tablecloths, copper pans on whitewashed walls, and beamed ceilings—the very definition of a trattoria. A wide selection of Italian favorites served in a casual setting. Early-bird specials and take-out service available. Open daily for lunch 11:30am–3:30pm and dinner 5:30pm–10:30pm. Major credit cards.

Tuscany $$$ *Bermuda House Lane, 95 Front Street, Hamilton; Tel: 292-4507.* A pizzeria and bar with a refined Florentine atmosphere right in the center of Hamilton. A good selection of Italian (especially Tuscan) favorites, with moderate prices. Eat indoors under Bermudian beam-and-slate ceilings or alfresco on the veranda overlooking Front Street. Dress is smart casual; reservations suggested. Open for lunch Monday–Friday 11:30am–2:30pm; dinner Monday–Saturday 6pm–10:30pm. Major credit cards.

Waterfront Tavern $$ *Somers Wharf, St. George's; Tel: 297-1515.* Casual dining in a waterside setting overlooking St. George's Harbour and the ship *Deliverance,* complete with large outside deck and stone-flagged interior. Fresh seafood and Bermudian dishes along with traditional pub fare. Open Monday–Saturday 10am–1am; Sunday noon–1am. Major credit cards.

Waterlot Inn $$$$ *101 South Shore Road, Southampton Parish; Tel: 238-8000.* This historic 300-year-old waterfront inn (now owned by the Fairmont Southampton Princess Hotel) features the finest in Mediterranean cuisine along with Bermudian favorites. New-world food served in an elegant old-world environment, complemented by a spectacular wine list. Formal dress required; reservations suggested. Open daily for dinner 6:30pm–9:30pm. Major credit cards.

INDEX

Berlitz Puts The World In Your Pocket

Berlitz speaks the language of travel. Its Pocket Guides take you to more than 110 destinations and its phrase books, pocket dictionaries, and cassette and CD language packs help you communicate when you get there.

Berlitz